Cooking with the

STARS & STRIPES

EVERYDAY RECIPES WITH DIETARY VARIATIONS

M L Rusenak

Copyright © 2023 by Trient Press

Trient Press
3375 S Rainbow Blvd
#81710, SMB 13135
Las Vegas,NV 89180
Ordering Information:
Quantity sales. Special discounts are available on quantity purchases by corporations, associations, and others. For details, contact the publisher at the address above.
Orders by U.S. trade bookstores and wholesalers. Please contact Trient Press: Tel: (775) 996-3844; or visit www.trientpress.com.
Printed in the United States of America

Publisher's Cataloging-in-Publication data
Ruscsak, M.L
A title of a book : Cooking with the Stars & Stripes

ISBN

Hard Cover   979-8-88990-014-6

Paper Back   979-8-88990-016-0

Ebook   979-8-88990-015-3

Welcome to 'Cooking with the Stars and Stripes,' a cookbook that offers everyday recipes with dietary variations. As the author of this cookbook, I bring to the table a unique combination of qualifications, having had the opportunity to study both the science and art of cooking.

My culinary journey started as a child when I discovered my love for baking. But it wasn't until I attended Lorain County Joint Vocational School in Oberlin, Ohio, that I truly found my passion for cooking. Under the guidance of Chef Michitsch and Chef Smith, I absorbed a wealth of knowledge that would later serve me in my own kitchen.

In 2012, I met the love of my life, but as fate would have it, I faced a dietary challenge. Creating a soy-free, dairy-free menu seemed like a daunting task. With my background in reading recipes and creating my own, I set out on a mission to find staple ingredients that would help me create delicious and healthy meals.

The search wasn't easy. I quickly discovered that 90% of processed foods contain soy or a soy derivative, and dairy can be found in even the most common household products like potato chips. But with my shopping list in hand, I persevered and compiled the recipes included in this book.

Each recipe has been tried and tested by me, with tweaks made to the "Base" recipe to make them soy-free, dairy-free, or both. The result is a collection of dishes that have reached a level of perfection that anyone can achieve.

So join me on this culinary adventure, and let's make everyday cooking easy, healthy, and delicious.

Dedication

For my daughter who needs directions on how to make mommy's awesome meals and sweets. And for anyone who loves to cook.

And for Chef Timothy Michitsch and Chef Smith from the L.C.J.V.S for showing me how to follow the recipes and how to make them my own.

Are you ready to take your baking and cooking to the next level? "Easy-to-Follow Baking and Cooking" is the cookbook for you! Whether you're a holiday baker or just a taste tester, this cookbook has something for everyone.

With variations for those with certain food allergies such as diabetes, lactose-free, gluten-free, and low-carb, you can create delicious treats without sacrificing taste or health. As someone with a family member who has food allergies, I understand the importance of having options for those with dietary restrictions. That's why I've included dairy-free and soy-sensitive variations with every recipe, which are also my core daily meals. Other variations are included by request from those who found out about this endeavor.

All of the recipes in this book have been tried and perfected in my own kitchen. So, you can trust that they're not only easy to follow but also delicious. And if you have any questions or need help with a step or variation, feel free to contact me on my Facebook page or website.

I even have some recipes with YouTube videos to help guide you through the process. You can find me at https://www.facebook.com/OfLiteAndDarke/ or https://www.doveanddragonpublishing.com/.

To make your baking and cooking experience even easier, I've included a list of brands that I use for variation. From soy-free mayo to gluten-free flour and pasta, these brands will help you make the perfect treat for any occasion.

So, get ready to impress your friends and family with your newfound baking and cooking skills. Order "Easy-to-Follow Baking and Cooking" today and let's get started on this delicious journey together!

Brands that I use for variation

Soy Free:
Mayo:
 Hampton Creek Just Mayo Mayonnaise
Follow Your Heart Vegenaise, Soy-Free
Spectrum Naturals Organic Mayonnaise with Olive Oil

Bread:
Angelic Sprouted Mash 7-Grain Bread
BFree Bread, Sandwich Loaf
Sara Lee Artesano Style Bread

Flour:
King Arthur Organic Unbleached All Purpose Flour
Bob's Red Mill Organic Flour
Miracle Flour- 100% Lupin Flour, Non-GMO, Gluten Free & Low Carb

Pasta:
Thrive Market Organic Fusilli
Thin Slim Foods

Breakfast

Shirred eggs

Egg in a basket

Eggs Benedict

Alternative Eggs Benedict

Pancakes

Classic Quiche Lorraine

Waffles

Omelettes

French toast

Smoothie bowls

Breakfast burritos

Breakfast casseroles

Frittatas

Breakfast sandwiches

Avocado toast

Homemade granola

Chia seed pudding

How many pleats are on a chef's hat? This was the first question asked on the first day of school my junior year of High school. The answer 101. Why is this important? 100 pleats represent the 100 ways to make an egg. A true chef knows all of them. Some, not all will be found here. Along with a few other breakfast ideas.

Shirred eggs

Also known as baked eggs, it is a dish in which eggs have been baked in a flat-bottomed dish; the name originates from the type of dish in which it was traditionally baked. An alternative way of cooking is to crack the eggs into individual ramekins and cook them in a water bath, creating the French dish eggs.

1/4 teaspoon softened butter
2 teaspoons heavy cream
2 eggs
salt and pepper to taste
1 teaspoon minced fresh chives
1 teaspoon grated Parmesan cheese

Preheat oven to 325 degrees F (165 degrees C).

Ready the center of the ramekin, then sprinkle with salt, pepper, chives, and Parmesan cheese.

Bake in preheated oven until the whites of the eggs have set and the yolks are still soft, 12 to 15 minutes. Remove from oven, and allow to set for 2 to 3 minutes before serving.
In

Rub the inside of a 6-ounce ramekin with butter. Pour cream into the ramekin, then crack the eggs on top of the cream without breaking the yolks. Use a spoon to position the yolks towards

Variation
Dairy free
Sub almond milk for heavy cream Add one egg
Omit cheese or use Daiya brand. Ask your grocer about availability

Egg in a basket

An egg fried within a hole in a slice of bread.

1 Egg
1 Bread
1 Toaster
1 Tablespoon Butter
Salt
Pepper
1 Frying Pan
1 Small glass or spray butter cap

Get one piece of lovely bread. The bigger the better.
Lightly toast your bread. This prevents soggy bread and helps cook bread faster. The cooking time of an egg is too short to attempt both at once. Plus, this gives a nice treat as you will see.

Cover side one in butter.

Now cover side two in butter. Important to do both sides & edges of bread because you will end up flipping the bread halfway through, the butter helps cook / not burn.

Now for the fun part. Take a small cup or a lid from a spray on butter can or something like that. Something about 2 - 2.5 inches in diameter works best.

Now cut a hole with the lid right through the middle of the bread.

Now take your pan, heat it up and place the bread in the pan with a teaspoon of butter in the middle.

Once the butter is nice and melted and starts to sizzle a little bit, it is time to bring in the egg

Now crack an egg right into the middle of the hole.

cook for about a minute and a half. Carefully lift up the edge and see if the bottom is nice and solid maybe a little bit of golden brownness.

Now flip it. You can see the egg has been cooked nicely on side one. The egg has cooked into the edges of the bread nicely. Again salt-and-pepper. Cook the second side about a minute or so.

Eggs Benedict

Poached eggs on Canadian bacon on top of toasted English muffin halves covered with hollandaise sauce.

4 egg yolks
3 1/2 tablespoons lemon juice
1 pinch ground white pepper
1/8 teaspoon Worcestershire sauce
1 tablespoon water
1 cup butter, melted
1/4 teaspoon salt
8 eggs
1 teaspoon distilled white vinegar
8 strips Canadian-style bacon
4 English muffins, split
2 tablespoons butter, softened
Prep

To Make Hollandaise: Fill the bottom of a double boiler part-way with water. Make sure that water does not touch the top pan. Bring water to a gentle simmer. In the top of the double boiler, whisk together egg yolks, lemon juice, white pepper, Worcestershire sauce, and 1 tablespoon water.

Add the melted butter to egg yolk mixture 1 or 2 tablespoons at a time while whisking yolks constantly. If hollandaise begins to get too thick, add a teaspoon or two of hot water. Continue whisking until all butter is incorporated. Whisk in salt, then remove from heat. Place a lid on pan to keep sauce warm.

Preheat oven on broiler setting. To Poach Eggs: Fill a large saucepan with 3 inches of water. Bring water to a gentle simmer, then add vinegar. Carefully break eggs into simmering water, and allow to cook for 2 1/2 to 3 minutes. Yolks should still be soft in center. Remove eggs from water with a slotted spoon and set on a warm plate.

While eggs are poaching, brown the bacon in a medium skillet over medium-high heat and toast the English muffins on a baking sheet under the broiler.

Spread toasted muffins with softened butter, and top each one with a slice of bacon, followed by one poached egg. Place 2 muffins on each plate and drizzle with hollandaise sauce. Sprinkle with chopped chives and serve immediately.

Variation

Real bacon or turkey bacon taste really good with this.
There are a few brands of Gluten free English muffins available check with your grocer for availability
EASY PALEO ENGLISH MUFFINS- low carb option is in chapter 5
Eggs Florentine- A variation of Eggs Benedict with spinach replacing Canadian bacon or it can be added to an additional flavor.

Alternative Eggs Benedict

8 pieces of bacon or 4 pieces of Canadian bacon
2 tablespoons chopped parsley, for garnish
4 eggs
2 teaspoons white or rice vinegar
2 English muffins
Butter
Blender Hollandaise

10 Tbsp unsalted butter
3 egg yolks
1 Tbsp lemon juice
1/2 teaspoon salt

Cook the bacon: Heat a large skillet on medium low heat. Add the strips of bacon or the slices of Canadian bacon. Slowly fry, turning occasionally, until the bacon is browned on both sides, and if using strip bacon, much of the fat is rendered out (about 10 minutes).

Use tongs or a fork to remove the bacon from the pan, set on a paper towel to absorb the excess fat.

Bring poaching water to a simmer: While the bacon is cooking, bring a large saucepan two-thirds-filled with water to a boil, then add the vinegar. Bring the water to a boil again, then lower the heat to a bare simmer.

Make Hollandaise sauce in blender: To make blender hollandaise, melt 10 Tbsp unsalted butter.

Put 3 egg yolks, a tablespoon of lemon juice, 1/2 teaspoon salt in a blender, blend on medium to medium high speed for 20-30 seconds, until eggs lighten in color.

Turn blender down to lowest setting, slowly dribble in the hot melted butter, while continuing to blend. Taste for salt and acidity and add more salt or lemon juice to taste.

Transfer it to a container you can use for pouring and set it on a warm—but not hot—place on or near the stovetop.

Poach the eggs: Here is an easy method for poaching eggs. Essentially, working one egg at a time you crack an egg into a small bowl and slip it into the barely simmering water. Once it begins to solidify, you can slip in another egg, until you have all four cooking.

Turn off the heat, cover the pan, and let sit for 4 minutes. (Remember which egg went in first, you'll want to take it out first.) When it comes time to remove the eggs, gently lift out with a slotted spoon.

Note that the timing is a little variable on the eggs, depending on the size of your pan, how much water, how many eggs, and how runny you like them. You might have to experiment a little with your set-up to figure out what you need to do to get the eggs exactly the way you like them.

Toast English muffins: As soon as all the eggs are in the poaching water, begin toasting your English muffins. If you can't get all the muffins toasted by the time the eggs are ready, gently remove the eggs from the poaching water and set in a bowl.

Assemble your Eggs Benedict: To assemble, butter one side of an English muffin. Top with two slices of bacon or 1 slice of Canadian bacon. You can trim the bacon to fit the muffin if you'd like.

Put a poached egg on top of the bacon, then pour some hollandaise over. Sprinkle some parsley over it all and serve at once.

Basic Omelette

with cheese, spinach, and mushrooms

Ingredients:

2 large eggs
1 tablespoon milk or water
Salt and pepper, to taste
1 tablespoon butter or oil
1/4 cup shredded cheese (cheddar, Swiss, or any other kind you like)
1/4 cup chopped fresh spinach
1/4 cup sliced mushrooms

Instructions:

In a small bowl, whisk together the eggs, milk or water, salt, and pepper until well combined.

Heat a non-stick skillet over medium-high heat. Add the butter or oil and let it melt.

Add the spinach and mushrooms to the skillet and sauté for 2-3 minutes, until the mushrooms are tender and the spinach is wilted.

Pour the egg mixture over the vegetables in the skillet. Let it cook for about 1 minute, or until the edges of the omelette start to set.

Using a spatula, gently lift the edges of the omelette and let the uncooked egg flow to the bottom of the skillet.

Once the top of the omelette is no longer runny, sprinkle the shredded cheese over one half of the omelette.

Use the spatula to fold the other half of the omelette over the cheese, creating a half-moon shape.

Cook the omelette for another minute, or until the cheese is melted and the eggs are cooked to your desired doneness.

Use the spatula to slide the omelette onto a plate and serve hot.

You can customize this recipe by adding or substituting other fillings such as ham, bacon, onions, peppers, or any other ingredients that you like in your omelettes. Enjoy!

French Toast

(with gluten-free bread for a variation)

Ingredients:

4 slices of bread (gluten-free, if desired)
2 large eggs
1/4 cup milk (or dairy-free alternative)
1/2 tsp vanilla extract
1/2 tsp ground cinnamon
1 tbsp butter (or dairy-free alternative)
Maple syrup, fruit, or other toppings of your choice

Instructions:

In a shallow bowl, whisk together the eggs, milk, vanilla extract, and cinnamon until well combined.
Heat a non-stick skillet or griddle over medium-high heat. Add the butter and let it melt.
Dip each slice of bread into the egg mixture, making sure to coat both sides.
Place the bread in the skillet and cook for 2-3 minutes on each side, or until golden brown.
Remove the French toast from the skillet and serve immediately with your desired toppings.
For a gluten-free variation, use gluten-free bread instead of regular bread. Make sure the bread is sturdy enough to hold up to the egg mixture and cooking process.

Pancakes

1 1/2 cups all-purpose flour
1 1/4 cups milk
1 egg
3 tablespoons butter, melted
3 1/2 teaspoons baking powder
1 teaspoon salt
1 tablespoon white sugar
1 teaspoon vanilla

Prep

In a large bowl, sift together the flour, baking powder, salt and sugar. Make a well in the center and pour in the milk, egg and melted butter; mix until smooth.

Heat a lightly oiled griddle or frying pan over medium high heat. Pour or scoop the batter onto the griddle, using approximately 1/4 cup for each pancake. Brown on both sides and serve hot.

Variation

Fresh fruit can be added to taste
Dairy free- Sub Almond milk for regular Milk
         Sub margin for butter
Diabetic friendly sub Splenda or your choice of sweetener for sugar
Gluten free and Low Carb- check with your grocer for availability in flour

Classic Quiche Lorraine

CRUST

1 cup all-purpose flour

1/4 teaspoon salt

1/3 cup cold Land O Lakes® Butter, cut into chunks

3 to 4 tablespoons cold water

FILLING

8 slices crisply cooked bacon, crumbled

1/3 cup chopped onion

4 (1 cup) ounces shredded Swiss cheese

2 cups Land O Lakes® Half & Half

4 large Land O Lakes® Eggs

1/4 teaspoon salt

1/8 teaspoon pepper

1/8 teaspoon ground nutmeg

Heat oven to 375°F.

Combine flour and 1/4 teaspoon salt in bowl; cut in butter with pastry blender or fork until mixture resembles coarse crumbs. Stir in enough water with fork; just until flour is moistened. Shape dough into a ball; flatten slightly.

Roll out dough on lightly floured surface into 12-inch circle. Fold into quarters. Carefully place pastry into ungreased 9-inch glass pie pan. Carefully unfold pastry, pressing firmly against bottom and sides of pie pan. Trim crust to 1/2 inch from edge of pan. Crimp or flute edge.

Sprinkle bacon onto crust; top with onion and cheese. Combine all remaining filling ingredients in bowl; beat with whisk until well mixed. Pour over cheese in pan.

Bake 40-45 minutes or until center is set. Let stand 10 minutes before cutting.

Variation

Dairy free: use Smart sense butter and Dialia cheese both are also soy free

For pork free sub with your favorite breakfast meat or veggies. This is wonderful with broccoli onions and spinach

Waffles

2 eggs
2 cups all-purpose flour
1 3/4 cups milk
1/2 cup vegetable oil
1 tablespoon white sugar
4 teaspoons baking powder
1/4 teaspoon salt

Preheat waffle iron. Beat eggs in large bowl with hand beater until fluffy. Beat in flour, milk, vegetable oil, sugar, baking powder, salt and vanilla, just until smooth.
Spray preheated waffle iron with non-stick cooking spray. Pour mix onto hot waffle iron. Cook until golden brown. Serve hot.

Variation
Dairy free: Use almond or cashew milk

Sugar free: Use Splenda or equal

Smoothie Bowls

with various fruit and granola toppings:

Ingredients:

2 cups frozen mixed berries
1 banana
1/2 cup Greek yogurt (or dairy-free alternative)
1/4 cup almond milk (or dairy-free alternative)
1 tbsp honey (or agave syrup)
1/2 cup granola
Assorted fresh fruit (such as sliced bananas, strawberries, kiwi, or blueberries)
Additional toppings, as desired (such as shredded coconut, chopped nuts, or chia seeds)

Instructions:

In a blender, combine the frozen berries, banana, Greek yogurt, almond milk, and honey. Blend until smooth and creamy.
Divide the smoothie mixture into 2-3 bowls.
Top each bowl with a generous spoonful of granola, along with assorted fresh fruit and additional toppings as desired.
Serve immediately and enjoy!
Feel free to experiment with different types of fruit or toppings to make this recipe your own. Enjoy your delicious and nutritious smoothie bowl!

Breakfast Burritos

with scrambled eggs, cheese, avocado, and salsa:

Ingredients:

4 large eggs
Salt and pepper, to taste
1 tbsp butter or oil
4 large flour tortillas
1/2 cup shredded cheddar cheese
1 ripe avocado, diced
1/4 cup salsa (or more, to taste)

Instructions:

In a large bowl, whisk together the eggs with salt and pepper to taste.

Heat the butter or oil in a non-stick skillet over medium heat.

Add the eggs and scramble until cooked through.

Warm the tortillas in the microwave or on a griddle.

Place a tortilla on a plate and add a quarter of the scrambled eggs, followed by a quarter of the shredded cheese, diced avocado, and salsa.

Roll the tortilla into a burrito by folding in the sides and rolling up tightly.

Repeat with the remaining tortillas and ingredients.

Serve immediately and enjoy!

Feel free to add additional ingredients such as diced tomatoes, sautéed onions or peppers, or cooked bacon or sausage to customize your breakfast burritos to your liking. Enjoy!

Breakfast Casserole
with Hash Browns, Sausage, Eggs, and Cheese:

Ingredients:

1 lb ground breakfast sausage
1 package (20 oz) frozen shredded hash browns, thawed
8 large eggs
1/2 cup milk (or dairy-free alternative)
1 tsp garlic powder
1 tsp onion powder
Salt and pepper, to taste
2 cups shredded cheddar cheese
Optional toppings: chopped green onions, sliced jalapeños, salsa, or hot sauce

Instructions:

Preheat your oven to 375°F (190°C) and grease a 9x13 inch baking dish.
In a large skillet, cook the ground breakfast sausage over medium heat until browned and cooked through.
Spread the thawed hash browns in the bottom of the prepared baking dish.
In a mixing bowl, whisk together the eggs, milk, garlic powder, onion powder, salt, and pepper until well combined.

Pour the egg mixture over the hash browns, then top with the cooked sausage and shredded cheese.

Bake for 35-40 minutes, or until the eggs are set and the cheese is melted and bubbly.

Remove from the oven and let cool for a few minutes before slicing into portions.

Serve hot with optional toppings as desired.

Enjoy your delicious and satisfying breakfast casserole! This recipe is perfect for feeding a crowd or meal prepping for the week.

Frittata

with Veggies, Cheese, and Herbs:

Ingredients:

8 large eggs
1/4 cup milk (or dairy-free alternative)
Salt and pepper, to taste
1 tbsp olive oil
1 small onion, diced
1 bell pepper, diced
1 zucchini, diced
1/2 cup shredded cheese (such as cheddar or mozzarella)
2 tbsp chopped fresh herbs (such as parsley, basil, or chives)

Instructions:

Preheat your oven to 350°F (175°C).

In a mixing bowl, whisk together the eggs, milk, salt, and pepper until well combined.

Heat the olive oil in a 10-inch oven-safe skillet over medium heat. Add the diced onion and bell pepper and sauté until softened, about 5 minutes.

Add the diced zucchini to the skillet and cook for an additional 2-3 minutes.

Pour the egg mixture over the vegetables in the skillet, then sprinkle with the shredded cheese and chopped herbs.

Transfer the skillet to the preheated oven and bake for 20-25 minutes, or until the frittata is set in the center and the cheese is melted and golden brown.

Remove from the oven and let cool for a few minutes before slicing into portions.

Serve hot or at room temperature, garnished with additional herbs if desired.

Feel free to add or substitute other veggies or herbs to make this frittata recipe your own. Enjoy!

Breakfast Sandwiches

Ingredients:

4 English muffins, split and toasted
4 large eggs
4 slices of cheddar or American cheese
4 slices of bacon or sausage patties
Salt and pepper, to taste
Butter or oil, for cooking

Instructions:

Cook the bacon or sausage in a skillet until crispy or cooked through, then set aside.

In a mixing bowl, whisk together the eggs with salt and pepper to taste.

Heat butter or oil in a non-stick skillet over medium heat. Add the egg mixture and scramble until cooked through.

To assemble the sandwiches, place a slice of cheese on the bottom half of each toasted English muffin. Add a quarter of the scrambled eggs, followed by a slice of cooked bacon or sausage.

Top with the other half of the English muffin.

Serve immediately and enjoy your delicious breakfast sandwiches!

Feel free to add additional ingredients such as sliced avocado, tomato, or sautéed onions and peppers to customize your breakfast sandwiches to your liking. Enjoy!

Avocado Toast

with Poached Eggs and Hot Sauce:

Ingredients:

2 slices of bread (such as sourdough or whole wheat)
1 ripe avocado, pitted and mashed
2 large eggs
1 tbsp white vinegar
Salt and pepper, to taste
Hot sauce, to taste

Instructions:

Toast the bread to your desired level of doneness.
While the bread is toasting, bring a pot of water to a boil and add the white vinegar.
Crack each egg into a separate small bowl or ramekin.
Reduce the heat of the pot of water so that it's simmering gently, then use a spoon to create a whirlpool in the water.
Gently pour each egg into the whirlpool, one at a time, and cook for 2-3 minutes for a soft yolk.
Remove the poached eggs with a slotted spoon and drain any excess water on a paper towel.
Spread the mashed avocado evenly on each slice of toasted bread. Season with salt and pepper to taste.
Place a poached egg on top of each slice of avocado toast.
Drizzle with hot sauce to taste.

Serve immediately and enjoy your delicious avocado toast with poached eggs and hot sauce!
Feel free to add other toppings like sliced tomatoes or crumbled bacon for extra flavor and texture. Enjoy!

Homemade Granola
with Oats, Nuts, and Dried Fruit:

Ingredients:

3 cups old-fashioned rolled oats
1 cup mixed nuts (such as almonds, walnuts, and pecans),
roughly chopped
1/2 cup unsweetened shredded coconut
1/4 cup honey or maple syrup
1/4 cup coconut oil or vegetable oil
1 tsp vanilla extract
1/2 tsp ground cinnamon
1/4 tsp salt
1 cup mixed dried fruit (such as raisins, cranberries, and
apricots), chopped

Instructions:

Preheat your oven to 325°F (165°C).

In a mixing bowl, combine the oats, mixed nuts, and shredded coconut.

In a small saucepan, heat the honey or maple syrup, coconut oil or vegetable oil, vanilla extract, ground cinnamon, and salt over low heat, stirring until well combined.

Pour the honey or maple syrup mixture over the oat mixture and stir until well coated.

Spread the granola mixture in an even layer on a large baking sheet.

Bake for 20-25 minutes, stirring halfway through, until golden brown and fragrant.

Remove from the oven and let cool for 5 minutes.

Add the chopped mixed dried fruit to the baking sheet and stir to combine.

Allow the granola to cool completely on the baking sheet before transferring it to an airtight container for storage.

Serve with your favorite yogurt, milk, or fruit for a tasty and nutritious breakfast or snack.

Feel free to customize this granola recipe to your liking by adding different nuts, spices, or dried fruits. Enjoy!

Chia Seed Pudding
with Coconut Milk and Fresh Fruit:

Ingredients:

1/2 cup chia seeds
2 cups coconut milk
1-2 tbsp honey or maple syrup (optional, for sweetness)
1 tsp vanilla extract
Fresh fruit, for serving (such as sliced berries, kiwi, mango, or banana)

Instructions:

In a mixing bowl, whisk together the chia seeds, coconut milk, honey or maple syrup (if using), and vanilla extract until well combined.

Cover the bowl and refrigerate for at least 2 hours, or preferably overnight, to allow the chia seeds to absorb the liquid and thicken into a pudding-like consistency.

Once the chia seed pudding is thickened to your desired consistency, give it a stir to break up any clumps and ensure that it's well mixed.

Divide the chia seed pudding into bowls or jars, and top with your desired fresh fruit.

Serve and enjoy your delicious and nutritious chia seed pudding!

Vegan Variations:

Vegan Breakfast Burrito: Fill a tortilla with scrambled tofu, avocado, salsa, and veggies such as bell peppers, onions, and spinach.

Vegan Pancakes: Mix together flour, baking powder, non-dairy milk, and a sweetener such as maple syrup or agave. Cook the batter on a griddle until golden brown.

Vegan Overnight Oats: Combine oats, non-dairy milk, chia seeds, and sweetener in a jar and let it sit in the fridge overnight. In the morning, add toppings such as fresh fruit, nuts, and seeds.

Vegan Tofu Scramble: Sauté crumbled tofu with veggies such as onions, bell peppers, and spinach, and season with spices such as turmeric, cumin, and paprika.

Vegan Smoothie Bowl: Blend together frozen fruit, non-dairy milk, and a protein source such as nut butter or protein powder. Top with granola, fresh fruit, and nuts.

Vegan Breakfast Sandwich: Toast an English muffin and top with a vegan sausage patty or tempeh bacon, sliced avocado, and a vegan cheese such as sliced vegan cheddar or cashew cheese.

Side Items

Rosemary Rice

2 cups rice. (For best results use Rosemary rice)

4 cups water

2 tbsp dry rosemary or one sprig fresh rosemary

1tbsp

Caraway seeds

2 tbsp condensed beef stock

½ stick butter or margarine

Sutea rosemary and caraway seeds in a large sauce pan.

Add dry rice and cook until translucent.

Add condensed beef tock

Cook until stock is mixed well with rice

Slowly add water ½ c at a time until rice is fully cooked.

Best paired with beef.

*** Variation***

Add diced onions or carrots for pilaf style rice

Sub ½ white wine for water near the end of cooking to give a bolder flavor

Little sausages

bottle barbeque sauce

1 cup packed brown sugar

1/2 cup ketchup

1 tablespoon Worcestershire sauce

1/3 cup chopped onion

2 (16 ounce) packages little wieners

Add all ingredients to list

Stir together barbecue sauce, brown sugar, ketchup, Worcestershire sauce, onion, and wieners in the bowl of a slow cooker. Cook on LOW for 2 hours, or until ready to serve.

Variation

Slow cooker little sausages

2 packs of lil sausages

1 tablespoon mustard

1/4 cup katup

1/4 cup brown sugar

1 small onion

Put all ingredients in slow cooker on low for minimum of two hours.

Splenda brown sugar can be substituted

This can be made with chicken tender loins. To do so adjust cooking time until the chicken is completely cooked. Stir occasionally.

Oven-Roasted Asparagus

1 bunch thin asparagus spears, trimmed

3 tablespoons olive oil

Bertolli Extra Light Tasting Olive Oil 25.5 Fl Oz

1 1/2 tablespoons grated Parmesan cheese (optional)

1 clove garlic, minced (optional)

1 teaspoon sea salt

1/2 teaspoon ground black pepper

1 tablespoon lemon juice (optional)

Preheat an oven to 425 degrees F (220 degrees C).

Place the asparagus into a mixing bowl, and drizzle with the olive oil. Toss to coat the spears, then sprinkle with Parmesan cheese, garlic, salt, and pepper. Arrange the asparagus onto a baking sheet in a single layer.

Bake in the preheated oven until just tender, 12 to 15 minutes depending on thickness. Sprinkle with lemon juice just before serving.

Brussels Sprouts with Bacon

1/2 pound bacon, diced

1 tablespoon extra-virgin olive oil

2 teaspoons butter

1/4 onion, diced

2 cloves garlic, minced

salt and black pepper to taste

1/2 cup balsamic vinegar1 1/2 pounds Brussels sprouts, trimmed and cut in half

2 cups chicken stock

Place the bacon in a large, deep skillet, and cook over medium-high heat, stirring occasionally, until evenly browned, but not crispy, about 10 minutes. Remove the bacon with a slotted spoon, leaving the grease in the skillet. Pour off all but 2 tablespoons of the bacon grease and stir in the olive oil, butter, onion, and garlic. Season with salt and pepper. Cook and stir until the onion softens and the garlic lightly browns, 5 to 7 minutes.

Stir in the balsamic vinegar and bring to a simmer; cook until the liquid has reduced by 1/3. Add the reserved bacon, the halved Brussels sprouts, and the chicken stock. Stir, then bring to a boil over high heat. Reduce heat to medium-low, and simmer until the Brussels sprouts are tender, yet still slightly firm, about 10 minutes

Candied Carrots

2 pounds carrots, cut into sticks

1/4 cup butter

1/4 cup packed brown sugar

1/4 teaspoon salt

1/8 teaspoon white pepper

Place carrots in a large saucepan; add 1 in. of water. Bring to a boil. Reduce heat; cover and simmer for 8-10 minutes or until crisp-tender. Drain and set aside.

In the same pan, combine the butter, brown sugar, salt and pepper; cook and stir until butter is melted. Return carrots to the pan; cook and stir over medium heat for 5 minutes or until glazed.

Variation:

Baby carrots are an easy alternative to cutting sticks

Smart sense Soy free dairy free butter works great with this

And Splenda Brown sugar makes for a diabetic friendly alternative

Twice Baked Potatoes

4 large baking potatoes

8 slices bacon

1 cup sour cream

1/2 cup milk

4 tablespoons butter

1/2 teaspoon salt

1/2 teaspoon pepper

Crushed Red Pepper Flakes

Bold and spicy addition to sauces and marinades.

1 cup shredded Cheddar cheese, divided

8 green onions, sliced, divided

Preheat oven to 350 degrees F (175 degrees C).

Bake potatoes in preheated oven for 1 hour.

Meanwhile, place bacon in a large, deep skillet. Cook over medium high heat until evenly brown. Drain, crumble and set aside.

When potatoes are done allow them to cool for 10 minutes. Slice potatoes in half lengthwise and scoop the flesh into a large bowl; save skins. To the potato flesh add sour cream, milk, butter, salt, pepper, 1/2 cup cheese and 1/2 the green onions. Mix with a hand mixer until well blended and creamy. Spoon the mixture into the potato skins. Top each with remaining cheese, green onions and bacon.

Bake for another 15 minutes.

Variation

Sub Smart sense Soy free dairy free butter, Omit the sour Cream and use Dialia cheese. This is still a wonderful recipe

Quinoa Salad

Ingredients

1 cup quinoa

2 cups water or vegetable broth

1 cucumber, diced

1 red bell pepper, diced

1 yellow bell pepper, diced

1 pint cherry tomatoes, halved

1/4 cup chopped fresh parsley or cilantro

1/4 cup olive oil

1/4 cup freshly squeezed lemon juice

Salt and pepper, to taste

Instructions:

Rinse the quinoa thoroughly in a fine-mesh strainer and drain well.

In a medium saucepan, bring the quinoa and water or broth to a boil. Reduce the heat to low and simmer for 15-20 minutes, or until the liquid is absorbed and the quinoa is tender.

Fluff the quinoa with a fork and transfer it to a large bowl.

Add the diced cucumber, bell peppers, cherry tomatoes, and chopped parsley or cilantro to the bowl with the quinoa.

In a small bowl, whisk together the olive oil, lemon juice, salt, and pepper. Pour the dressing over the quinoa salad and toss to combine.

Chill the quinoa salad in the refrigerator for at least 30 minutes before serving.

Serve cold and enjoy!

This recipe can be easily customized to suit different tastes and dietary needs. You can add or substitute different vegetables, herbs, or spices, and adjust the amount of dressing to your liking. It can also be made vegan or vegetarian, and is naturally gluten-free and nut-free.

Roasted Root Vegetables

Ingredients:

2 large carrots, peeled and chopped into 1-inch pieces

2 medium sweet potatoes, peeled and chopped into 1-inch pieces

2 medium parsnips, peeled and chopped into 1-inch pieces

2 medium beets, peeled and chopped into 1-inch pieces

2 tablespoons olive oil

1 teaspoon dried thyme

1 teaspoon dried rosemary

Salt and pepper, to taste

Instructions:

Preheat the oven to 400°F (200°C).

In a large mixing bowl, combine the chopped carrots, sweet potatoes, parsnips, and beets.

Drizzle the olive oil over the vegetables, then sprinkle the dried thyme and rosemary on top. Add salt and pepper to taste, and toss everything together until the vegetables are evenly coated.

Transfer the vegetables to a baking sheet in a single layer.

Roast the vegetables in the preheated oven for 25-30 minutes, or until they are tender and slightly caramelized, stirring once halfway through.

Remove from the oven and serve immediately.

This recipe is easy to customize by using different root vegetables or herbs to suit your preferences. It can also be made vegan, vegetarian, and gluten-free.

Roasted Garlic Mashed Cauliflower

Ingredients:

1 head of cauliflower, chopped into florets

1 head of garlic

1 tablespoon olive oil

1/4 cup non-dairy milk (such as almond, soy, or oat milk)

2 tablespoons vegan butter or olive oil

Salt and pepper, to taste

Fresh chives or parsley, for garnish (optional)

Instructions:

Preheat the oven to 400°F (200°C).

Cut off the top of the garlic head to expose the cloves. Drizzle with olive oil and wrap in foil. Roast in the preheated oven for 30-35 minutes, or until the garlic is soft and fragrant.

Meanwhile, steam the cauliflower florets in a steamer basket over boiling water until tender, about 10-15 minutes.

Drain the cauliflower and transfer it to a mixing bowl. Mash the cauliflower with a potato masher or fork until smooth.

Squeeze the roasted garlic cloves out of their skins and add them to the mashed cauliflower, along with the non-dairy milk and vegan butter or olive oil. Mix well.

Season with salt and pepper to taste.

Transfer the mashed cauliflower to a serving dish and garnish with fresh chives or parsley, if desired.

Serve immediately.

This recipe is a delicious and healthy alternative to traditional mashed potatoes, and it can be customized to suit different dietary needs. It's vegan, vegetarian, gluten-free, and low-carb.

Baked Sweet Potato Fries

Ingredients:

2 medium sweet potatoes, peeled and cut into fry-shaped pieces

2 tablespoons olive oil

1 teaspoon paprika

1/2 teaspoon cumin

1/2 teaspoon salt

Freshly ground black pepper, to taste

Instructions:

Preheat the oven to 400°F (200°C).

In a large bowl, toss the sweet potato fries with the olive oil, paprika, cumin, salt, and pepper until well-coated.

Spread the sweet potato fries in a single layer on a baking sheet lined with parchment paper.

Bake in the preheated oven for 20-25 minutes, or until crispy and golden brown, flipping the fries halfway through.

Remove from the oven and serve immediately.

These baked sweet potato fries are a healthier and more flavorful alternative to regular french fries. They're vegan, vegetarian, gluten-free, and nut-free, so they can be enjoyed by people with various dietary restrictions. You can also experiment with different spices and seasonings to customize the flavor to your liking. Enjoy!

Grilled Portobello Mushrooms:

Ingredients:

4 large portobello mushrooms, stems removed

1/4 cup balsamic vinegar

2 tablespoons olive oil

2 garlic cloves, minced

1 tablespoon fresh thyme leaves

1 tablespoon fresh rosemary leaves, chopped

Salt and pepper, to taste

Instructions:

In a large bowl, whisk together the balsamic vinegar, olive oil, garlic, thyme, rosemary, salt, and pepper.

Add the portobello mushrooms to the bowl and toss to coat in the marinade. Let marinate for at least 30 minutes, or up to 2 hours in the refrigerator.

Preheat the grill to medium-high heat.

Grill the portobello mushrooms for 4-5 minutes per side, or until tender and slightly charred.

Remove the mushrooms from the grill and let cool for a few minutes before serving.

These grilled portobello mushrooms make a delicious and satisfying vegetarian or vegan main course. They're also gluten-free and nut-free, making them a great option for people with food allergies or intolerances. Serve them with a side salad or roasted vegetables for a complete meal. Enjoy!

Truffle Mashed Potatoes

Ingredients:

2 pounds potatoes, peeled and diced

1/4 cup unsalted butter, at room temperature

1/4 cup heavy cream, at room temperature

1 tablespoon truffle oil, or more to taste

Salt and pepper, to taste

Chopped chives, for garnish

Instructions:

Place the diced potatoes in a large pot and cover with cold water. Add a pinch of salt to the water.

Bring the water to a boil and cook the potatoes until they are fork-tender, about 15-20 minutes.

Drain the potatoes and return them to the pot.

Add the butter and heavy cream to the pot and mash the potatoes with a potato masher until smooth and creamy.

Stir in the truffle oil and season with salt and pepper to taste.

Transfer the mashed potatoes to a serving bowl and sprinkle with chopped chives for garnish.

These Truffle Mashed Potatoes are a decadent and flavorful side dish that will impress your guests. They're perfect for special occasions or holidays, and can be made vegetarian, gluten-free, and nut-free. Serve them alongside roasted meats, grilled vegetables, or a hearty salad. Enjoy!

Lobster Mac and Cheese

Ingredients:

1 pound elbow macaroni (gluten-free, if desired)

1/2 cup unsalted butter

1/2 cup all-purpose flour (or gluten-free flour blend)

4 cups milk (or non-dairy milk)

2 cups shredded cheddar cheese

1 cup shredded gruyere cheese

1/2 teaspoon garlic powder

Salt and pepper to taste

1 pound cooked lobster meat, chopped into bite-sized pieces

1/4 cup chopped fresh parsley

Instructions:

Preheat oven to 375°F (190°C).

Cook the macaroni according to package instructions until al dente. Drain and set aside.

In a large saucepan, melt the butter over medium heat. Whisk in the flour until smooth and cook for 2-3 minutes.

Gradually whisk in the milk and cook, whisking constantly, until the mixture thickens and comes to a simmer.

Stir in the cheddar cheese, gruyere cheese, garlic powder, salt, and pepper until the cheese is melted and the sauce is smooth.

Add the cooked macaroni and lobster meat to the sauce and stir until well combined.

Transfer the mixture to a greased 9x13 inch baking dish and bake for 25-30 minutes, until bubbly and golden brown on top.

Let the mac and cheese cool for a few minutes before serving. Garnish with chopped parsley and serve hot.

Enjoy your delicious and decadent Lobster Mac and Cheese!

*** please note this is a family favorite however is the only recipe in this collect I have not made nor ate. ***

Grilled Asparagus with Hollandaise Sauce

Ingredients:

1 lb asparagus, trimmed

2 tbsp olive oil

Salt and pepper

3 egg yolks

1 tbsp lemon juice

1/2 cup unsalted butter, melted

Salt and pepper, to taste

Lemon wedges, for serving

Instructions:

Preheat grill to medium-high heat.

Toss the trimmed asparagus with olive oil, salt, and pepper.

Grill asparagus for 5-7 minutes or until tender and lightly charred.

While the asparagus is cooking, make the hollandaise sauce. In a heatproof bowl, whisk together the egg yolks and lemon juice until smooth.

Place the bowl over a pot of simmering water, making sure the bottom of the bowl doesn't touch the water.

Gradually pour in the melted butter while whisking constantly until the sauce is thick and smooth.

Remove the bowl from the heat and season the sauce with salt and pepper to taste.

Serve the grilled asparagus with the hollandaise sauce and lemon wedges on the side.

Note: To make this recipe gluten-free, be sure to use a gluten-free hollandaise sauce or make your own using gluten-free ingredients.

Roasted Beet and Goat Cheese Salad

Ingredients:

3-4 medium-sized beets, roasted and sliced

4 cups arugula

1/2 cup crumbled goat cheese

1/4 cup chopped toasted walnuts

2 tablespoons balsamic vinegar

1 tablespoon honey

1 tablespoon Dijon mustard

1/4 cup olive oil

Salt and pepper, to taste

Instructions:

Preheat oven to 400°F. Wash beets and remove stems and roots. Wrap each beet individually in aluminum foil and place on a baking sheet. Roast for 45-60 minutes or until beets are tender when pierced with a fork. Let cool, then remove skins and slice into wedges.

In a small bowl, whisk together balsamic vinegar, honey, and Dijon mustard. Slowly add in olive oil, whisking until emulsified. Season with salt and pepper to taste.

In a large bowl, toss arugula with half of the dressing. Arrange beets on top of the arugula and drizzle with the remaining dressing. Sprinkle goat cheese and toasted walnuts over the top.

Serve immediately and enjoy!

Roasted Brussels Sprouts with Bacon Jam

Ingredients:

1 lb Brussels sprouts, trimmed and halved

2 tbsp olive oil

Salt and pepper, to taste

4 slices bacon, diced

1 onion, diced

2 cloves garlic, minced

2 tbsp balsamic vinegar

1/4 cup maple syrup

1/4 tsp red pepper flakes (optional)

Instructions:

Preheat the oven to 400°F (200°C).

In a large bowl, toss the Brussels sprouts with olive oil, salt, and pepper.

Spread the Brussels sprouts in a single layer on a baking sheet and roast for 25-30 minutes, or until tender and crispy.

Meanwhile, in a large skillet over medium heat, cook the bacon until crispy. Remove the bacon from the skillet and drain on paper towels.

Add the onion to the skillet and cook until caramelized, about 10-12 minutes.

Add the garlic and cook for another minute.

Add the balsamic vinegar, maple syrup, and red pepper flakes (if using) to the skillet and bring to a simmer.

Reduce the heat and simmer until the mixture has thickened, about 10 minutes.

Stir in the cooked bacon and remove from heat.

Serve the roasted Brussels sprouts with the bacon jam on top.

Enjoy your delicious and savory Roasted Brussels Sprouts with Bacon Jam!

Sauces

Marinara Sauce

Alfredo Sauce

Pesto Sauce

Bechamel Sauce

Hollandaise Sauce

Aioli Sauce

BBQ Sauce

Chimichurri Sauce

Teriyaki Sauce

Satay Sauce

Cranberry Sauce

Harissa Sauce

Romesco Sauce

Remoulade Sauce

Hoisin Sauce

Tahini Sauce

Green Goddess Sauce

Sriracha Sauce

Mango Salsa Sauce

Chocolate Ganache Sauce

Salted Caramel Sauce

Raspberry Sauce

Lemon Curd Sauce

Vanilla Custard Sauce

Strawberry Sauce

Marinara Sauce:

Ingredients:

2 tablespoons olive oil

1 onion, finely chopped

3 cloves garlic, minced

1 can (28 oz) crushed tomatoes

1 teaspoon dried oregano

1 teaspoon dried basil

1/2 teaspoon salt

1/4 teaspoon black pepper

Optional: red pepper flakes for heat, fresh chopped parsley for garnish

Instructions:

In a medium saucepan, heat the olive oil over medium heat. Add the finely chopped onion and sauté until translucent, about 5 minutes.

Add the minced garlic to the pot and sauté for another 1-2 minutes, until fragrant.

Add the crushed tomatoes, dried oregano, dried basil, salt, and black pepper to the pot. Stir well to combine.

Bring the sauce to a boil, then reduce the heat and let simmer for 20-30 minutes, stirring occasionally, until the sauce has thickened.

Optional: add red pepper flakes for a spicy kick and fresh chopped parsley for added flavor and garnish.

Serve the marinara sauce hot over pasta, as a dipping sauce for bread, or use as a base for pizza sauce.

Enjoy your delicious and easy-to-make Marinara Sauce!

Alfredo Sauce:

Ingredients:

1/2 cup unsalted butter

1 cup heavy cream

1/2 teaspoon garlic powder

1/2 teaspoon salt

1/4 teaspoon black pepper

1 1/2 cups freshly grated Parmesan cheese

Optional: fresh chopped parsley for garnish

Instructions:

In a medium saucepan, melt the unsalted butter over medium heat.

Add the heavy cream to the pan and stir well to combine with the melted butter.

Add the garlic powder, salt, and black pepper to the pan and stir well to combine.

Reduce the heat to low and let the sauce simmer for 5-10 minutes, stirring occasionally.

Add the freshly grated Parmesan cheese to the pan and stir well to combine. The cheese will melt and the sauce will thicken as you stir.

Continue to stir the sauce until it reaches the desired thickness. If the sauce is too thick, you can add a little more heavy cream to thin it out.

Optional: garnish the Alfredo sauce with fresh chopped parsley for added flavor and presentation.

Serve the Alfredo sauce hot over pasta or use as a dipping sauce for breadsticks.

Pesto Sauce:

Ingredients:

2 cups fresh basil leaves, packed

1/2 cup freshly grated Parmesan cheese

1/2 cup extra-virgin olive oil

1/3 cup pine nuts or walnuts

3 garlic cloves, peeled

1/2 teaspoon salt

1/4 teaspoon black pepper

Instructions:

In a food processor, combine the fresh basil leaves, freshly grated Parmesan cheese, pine nuts or walnuts, garlic cloves, salt, and black pepper.

Pulse the ingredients together until they are roughly chopped and combined.

With the food processor running, slowly pour in the extra-virgin olive oil through the top of the food processor until the mixture is smooth and fully combined.

Taste the pesto sauce and adjust the seasoning as needed, adding more salt or black pepper to taste.

Optional: If the pesto sauce is too thick, you can add a little more olive oil to thin it out.

Serve the pesto sauce immediately over pasta, as a topping for grilled meats or vegetables, or use as a spread for sandwiches or bruschetta.

Bechamel Sauce:

Ingredients:

4 tablespoons unsalted butter

4 tablespoons all-purpose flour

2 cups whole milk

1/4 teaspoon ground nutmeg

1/2 teaspoon salt

1/4 teaspoon black pepper

Instructions:

In a medium saucepan, melt the unsalted butter over medium heat.

Add the all-purpose flour to the pan and whisk until the mixture is smooth and combined.

Cook the flour mixture, stirring constantly, for 2-3 minutes until it turns golden brown in color.

Slowly pour the whole milk into the pan, whisking constantly to avoid lumps. Continue to whisk until the mixture is smooth and well combined.

Add the ground nutmeg, salt, and black pepper to the pan and whisk until they are fully incorporated.

Reduce the heat to low and let the Bechamel sauce simmer for 5-10 minutes, stirring occasionally, until it thickens to your desired consistency.

Taste the Bechamel sauce and adjust the seasoning as needed, adding more salt or black pepper to taste.

Serve the Bechamel sauce immediately as a base for white pasta sauces or as a topping for vegetables or meat dishes.

Hollandaise Sauce:

Ingredients:

3 egg yolks

1 tablespoon lemon juice

1/2 cup unsalted butter, melted and hot

1/4 teaspoon salt

1/4 teaspoon cayenne pepper (optional)

Instructions:

Fill a saucepan with a couple of inches of water and heat it over medium heat until it simmers.

In a heatproof bowl that can fit over the saucepan without touching the water, whisk together the egg yolks and lemon juice until they are well combined.

Place the bowl over the simmering water and whisk constantly for 3-4 minutes, or until the mixture thickens and forms ribbons.

Remove the bowl from the heat and slowly pour the melted butter into the egg mixture, whisking constantly until the mixture becomes thick and creamy.

Add the salt and cayenne pepper (if using) and whisk until they are fully incorporated.

Taste the Hollandaise sauce and adjust the seasoning as needed, adding more salt or lemon juice to taste.

Serve the Hollandaise sauce immediately over poached eggs, grilled vegetables, or grilled fish.

Aioli Sauce:

Ingredients:

2 cloves garlic, finely chopped

1/2 teaspoon salt

1/2 teaspoon Dijon mustard

2 egg yolks

1 tablespoon lemon juice

1 cup olive oil

Instructions:

In a small bowl, mash the finely chopped garlic and salt together with a fork until it forms a smooth paste.

Add the Dijon mustard to the bowl and stir until it is fully incorporated into the garlic paste.

In a separate bowl, whisk together the egg yolks and lemon juice until they are well combined.

Slowly pour the olive oil into the egg mixture, whisking constantly, until the mixture thickens and forms a creamy emulsion.

Once the emulsion has formed, slowly whisk in the garlic and Dijon mustard paste, stirring constantly, until it is fully incorporated into the aioli.

Taste the aioli and adjust the seasoning as needed, adding more salt or lemon juice to taste.

Cover the aioli and refrigerate it for at least 30 minutes before serving to allow the flavors to meld together.

Serve the aioli as a dip for vegetables, as a spread for sandwiches, or as a condiment for grilled meats or fish.

BBQ Sauce:

Ingredients:

1 cup ketchup

1/2 cup apple cider vinegar

1/4 cup brown sugar

1/4 cup molasses

1 tablespoon Worcestershire sauce

1 teaspoon smoked paprika

1 teaspoon garlic powder

1/2 teaspoon onion powder

1/2 teaspoon salt

1/4 teaspoon black pepper

Instructions:

In a medium-sized saucepan, combine the ketchup, apple cider vinegar, brown sugar, molasses, Worcestershire sauce, smoked paprika, garlic powder, onion powder, salt, and black pepper.

Whisk the ingredients together until they are well combined and the brown sugar has dissolved.

Place the saucepan over medium heat and bring the mixture to a simmer.

Reduce the heat to low and let the BBQ sauce simmer for 10-15 minutes, stirring occasionally, until it thickens and the flavors have melded together.

Taste the BBQ sauce and adjust the seasoning as needed, adding more salt or sugar to taste.

Remove the BBQ sauce from the heat and let it cool for a few minutes before transferring it to a clean jar or container.

Store the BBQ sauce in the refrigerator for up to two weeks.

Chimichurri Sauce:

Ingredients:

1 cup fresh parsley leaves, chopped

1/2 cup fresh cilantro leaves, chopped

4 cloves garlic, minced

1/4 cup red wine vinegar

1/2 teaspoon salt

1/4 teaspoon black pepper

1/2 teaspoon red pepper flakes (optional)

1/2 cup extra-virgin olive oil

Instructions:

In a small mixing bowl, combine the chopped parsley, cilantro, minced garlic, red wine vinegar, salt, black pepper, and red pepper flakes (if using). Stir well to combine.

Slowly drizzle in the olive oil while whisking constantly. Continue whisking until the sauce is emulsified and well combined.

Taste the sauce and adjust the seasoning as needed, adding more salt, black pepper, or red pepper flakes to taste.

Cover the bowl with plastic wrap and refrigerate the Chimichurri sauce for at least 30 minutes to allow the flavors to meld together.

Serve the Chimichurri sauce with grilled meats, vegetables, or as a dipping sauce for bread.

Teriyaki Sauce:

Ingredients:

1/2 cup soy sauce

1/4 cup brown sugar

1/4 cup honey

1/4 cup rice vinegar

1 teaspoon minced garlic

1 teaspoon grated ginger

1 tablespoon cornstarch

2 tablespoons water

Instructions:

In a medium-sized saucepan, combine the soy sauce, brown sugar, honey, rice vinegar, minced garlic, and grated ginger. Stir well to combine.

Place the saucepan over medium heat and bring the mixture to a simmer.

In a small bowl, whisk together the cornstarch and water until the cornstarch is fully dissolved.

Slowly pour the cornstarch mixture into the simmering Teriyaki sauce while whisking constantly.

Reduce the heat to low and let the Teriyaki sauce simmer for 5-10 minutes, stirring occasionally, until it has thickened and the flavors have melded together.

Remove the Teriyaki sauce from the heat and let it cool for a few minutes before transferring it to a clean jar or container.

Store the Teriyaki sauce in the refrigerator for up to two weeks.

Satay Sauce:

Ingredients:

1 cup smooth peanut butter

1/4 cup soy sauce

1/4 cup brown sugar

2 tablespoons lime juice

2 teaspoons minced garlic

1 teaspoon grated ginger

1/4 teaspoon cayenne pepper

1/2 cup water

Instructions:

In a medium-sized saucepan, combine the peanut butter, soy sauce, brown sugar, lime juice, minced garlic, grated ginger, and cayenne pepper. Stir well to combine.

Gradually whisk in the water, stirring constantly, until the sauce is smooth and well combined.

Place the saucepan over medium heat and bring the Satay sauce to a simmer.

Reduce the heat to low and let the Satay sauce simmer for 5-10 minutes, stirring occasionally, until it has thickened and the flavors have melded together.

Remove the Satay sauce from the heat and let it cool for a few minutes before transferring it to a clean jar or container.

Store the Satay sauce in the refrigerator for up to two weeks.

Enjoy your delicious Satay sauce! It is perfect as a dipping sauce for skewered meats, vegetables, or tofu. You can also use it as a marinade or as a sauce for noodles or stir-fry dishes.

Cranberry Sauce:

Ingredients:

1 bag (12 ounces) of fresh or frozen cranberries

1 cup of granulated sugar

1 cup of water

1 tablespoon of orange zest

1 cinnamon stick (optional)

Instructions:

Rinse the cranberries with cold water and discard any damaged or bruised ones.

In a medium saucepan, combine the cranberries, sugar, water, orange zest, and cinnamon stick (if using) over medium-high heat.

Bring the mixture to a boil, stirring occasionally to dissolve the sugar. Reduce the heat to medium-low and let the mixture simmer for 10-15 minutes, until the cranberries have popped and the sauce has thickened.

Remove the cinnamon stick from the sauce and discard.

If you prefer a smoother sauce, you can use an immersion blender to puree the sauce until it's smooth. Be careful not to over-blend, as you want to keep some texture to the sauce.

Let the sauce cool to room temperature, then transfer it to a container with a lid and store it in the refrigerator for up to 1 week.

Serve the cranberry sauce chilled or at room temperature alongside your favorite holiday dishes.

Harissa Sauce:

Ingredients:

6-8 dried red chili peppers, stemmed and seeded

1 teaspoon of cumin seeds

1 teaspoon of coriander seeds

1 teaspoon of caraway seeds

3-4 garlic cloves, peeled

2 tablespoons of tomato paste

1 tablespoon of lemon juice

1/4 cup of olive oil

1/2 teaspoon of salt

Instructions:

In a dry skillet over medium heat, toast the chili peppers, cumin seeds, coriander seeds, and caraway seeds until fragrant, about 2-3 minutes. Remove from heat and let cool.

Once cool, add the toasted spices and chili peppers to a food processor along with the garlic cloves, tomato paste, lemon juice, olive oil, and salt.

Process the mixture until smooth, scraping down the sides as needed.

Taste the harissa sauce and adjust seasoning if needed.

Transfer the sauce to a jar with a tight-fitting lid and store in the refrigerator for up to 1 week.

Harissa sauce is a versatile condiment that can be used as a dip, marinade, or seasoning for grilled meats and vegetables, roasted potatoes, sandwiches, and more. Enjoy!

Romesco Sauce:

Ingredients:

1/2 cup of roasted almonds

1/2 cup of roasted hazelnuts

2 roasted red bell peppers, seeded and peeled

3 garlic cloves, peeled

1/4 cup of chopped fresh parsley

1 tablespoon of red wine vinegar

1 teaspoon of smoked paprika

1/4 teaspoon of cayenne pepper

1/2 cup of olive oil

Salt and freshly ground black pepper to taste

Instructions:

Preheat your oven to 350°F. Spread the almonds and hazelnuts on a baking sheet and roast for 8-10 minutes, or until lightly browned and fragrant.

Remove the nuts from the oven and let them cool for a few minutes. Once cool enough to handle, transfer the nuts to a clean kitchen towel and rub them to remove as much of the skins as possible.

In a food processor or blender, combine the roasted nuts, roasted red bell peppers, garlic cloves, parsley, red wine vinegar, smoked paprika, and cayenne pepper.

Pulse the mixture until it's finely chopped but still has some texture.

With the motor running, slowly drizzle in the olive oil until the sauce is smooth and creamy. If the sauce is too thick, you can add more olive oil until it reaches the desired consistency.

Season the romesco sauce with salt and freshly ground black pepper to taste.

Transfer the sauce to a jar with a tight-fitting lid and store in the refrigerator for up to 1 week.

Romesco sauce is a traditional Spanish sauce that's perfect for serving with grilled meats, roasted vegetables, fish, and more. Enjoy!

Remoulade Sauce:

Ingredients:

1 cup of mayonnaise

1/4 cup of Dijon mustard

2 tablespoons of chopped fresh parsley

2 tablespoons of chopped green onions

2 tablespoons of capers, drained and chopped

1 tablespoon of minced garlic

1 tablespoon of fresh lemon juice

1 teaspoon of paprika

1/2 teaspoon of hot sauce (such as Tabasco)

Salt and freshly ground black pepper to taste

Instructions:

In a medium bowl, whisk together the mayonnaise, Dijon mustard, chopped parsley, chopped green onions, capers, minced garlic, fresh lemon juice, paprika, and hot sauce until well combined.

Taste the remoulade sauce and season with salt and freshly ground black pepper to taste.

Cover the bowl with plastic wrap and refrigerate for at least 30 minutes to allow the flavors to meld together.

Serve the remoulade sauce chilled as a condiment or dipping sauce for fried seafood, vegetables, sandwiches, and more.

Remoulade sauce is a classic French sauce that's popular in Cajun and Creole cuisine. It's a delicious and versatile condiment that adds a tangy, spicy kick to any dish. Enjoy!

Hoisin Sauce:

Ingredients:

1/4 cup of soy sauce

2 tablespoons of black bean paste

2 tablespoons of honey

1 tablespoon of rice vinegar

1 tablespoon of toasted sesame oil

2 garlic cloves, minced

1 teaspoon of Chinese five-spice powder

Instructions:

In a small bowl, whisk together the soy sauce, black bean paste, honey, rice vinegar, toasted sesame oil, minced garlic, and Chinese five-spice powder until well combined.

Taste the hoisin sauce and adjust seasoning if needed.

Transfer the hoisin sauce to a jar with a tight-fitting lid and store in the refrigerator for up to 1 week.

Hoisin sauce is a sweet and savory sauce that's commonly used in Chinese cuisine as a dipping sauce, marinade, or condiment. It's particularly delicious with grilled meats, stir-fries, and dumplings. Enjoy!

Tahini Sauce:

Ingredients:

1/2 cup of tahini paste

1/4 cup of water

3 tablespoons of fresh lemon juice

2 garlic cloves, minced

1/2 teaspoon of ground cumin

1/4 teaspoon of cayenne pepper

Salt and freshly ground black pepper to taste

Instructions:

In a small bowl, whisk together the tahini paste, water, fresh lemon juice, minced garlic, ground cumin, and cayenne pepper until smooth and creamy.

If the sauce is too thick, you can add more water, 1 tablespoon at a time, until it reaches the desired consistency.

Taste the tahini sauce and season with salt and freshly ground black pepper to taste.

Transfer the tahini sauce to a serving bowl and drizzle with a little bit of olive oil, if desired.

Tahini sauce is a delicious and versatile condiment that's commonly used in Middle Eastern cuisine. It's particularly delicious as a dipping sauce for falafel, grilled meats, and vegetables, or as a dressing for salads. Enjoy!

Green Goddess Sauce:

Ingredients:

1/2 cup of mayonnaise

1/2 cup of sour cream

1/4 cup of chopped fresh parsley

1/4 cup of chopped fresh chives

2 tablespoons of chopped fresh tarragon

2 tablespoons of fresh lemon juice

1 garlic clove, minced

Salt and freshly ground black pepper to taste

Instructions:

In a medium bowl, whisk together the mayonnaise, sour cream, chopped parsley, chopped chives, chopped tarragon, fresh lemon juice, and minced garlic until well combined.

Taste the green goddess sauce and season with salt and freshly ground black pepper to taste.

Cover the bowl with plastic wrap and refrigerate for at least 30 minutes to allow the flavors to meld together.

Serve the green goddess sauce chilled as a dressing for salads, a dip for vegetables or chips, or as a condiment for grilled meats and seafood.

Green goddess sauce is a classic dressing that's full of fresh herbs and tangy flavors. It's a delicious and versatile sauce that can be used in a variety of dishes. Enjoy!

Sriracha Sauce:

Ingredients:

1 pound of fresh red jalapeño peppers, stemmed and roughly chopped

1/2 cup of distilled white vinegar

1/2 cup of granulated sugar

3 garlic cloves, minced

1 teaspoon of salt

Instructions:

In a medium saucepan, combine the chopped jalapeño peppers, distilled white vinegar, granulated sugar, minced garlic, and salt. Bring the mixture to a boil over medium-high heat.

Reduce the heat to medium-low and simmer the sauce, stirring occasionally, for 10-15 minutes or until the peppers are very soft and the mixture has thickened.

Remove the saucepan from the heat and let the mixture cool slightly.

Transfer the mixture to a blender or food processor and puree until smooth and creamy.

If the sauce is too thick, you can add a little bit of water, 1 tablespoon at a time, until it reaches the desired consistency.

Taste the sriracha sauce and adjust seasoning if needed.

Transfer the sriracha sauce to a jar with a tight-fitting lid and store in the refrigerator for up to 1 month.

Sriracha sauce is a spicy and tangy condiment that's commonly used in Southeast Asian cuisine as a dipping sauce, marinade, or condiment. It's particularly delicious with grilled meats, stir-fries, and noodle dishes. Enjoy!

Mango Salsa Sauce:

Ingredients:

2 ripe mangoes, peeled and diced

1 red bell pepper, seeded and diced

1/2 red onion, diced

1 jalapeño pepper, seeded and minced

1/4 cup of chopped fresh cilantro

2 tablespoons of fresh lime juice

1 tablespoon of honey

Salt and freshly ground black pepper to taste

Instructions:

In a medium bowl, combine the diced mangoes, diced red bell pepper, diced red onion, minced jalapeño pepper, and chopped cilantro.

In a separate small bowl, whisk together the fresh lime juice and honey until well combined.

Pour the lime and honey mixture over the mango mixture and stir until the ingredients are well combined.

Season the mango salsa sauce with salt and freshly ground black pepper to taste.

Cover the bowl with plastic wrap and refrigerate for at least 30 minutes to allow the flavors to meld together.

Serve the mango salsa sauce chilled as a dip for tortilla chips, or as a topping for grilled meats, seafood, or tacos.

Mango salsa sauce is a delicious and refreshing sauce that's perfect for adding a tropical twist to your favorite dishes. It's particularly delicious with grilled meats and seafood, or as a topping for tacos and burritos. Enjoy!

Chocolate Ganache Sauce

Ingredients:

8 ounces of high-quality semisweet chocolate, chopped into small pieces

1 cup of heavy cream

1 tablespoon of unsalted butter

1 teaspoon of pure vanilla extract

Pinch of salt

Instructions:

Place the chopped chocolate pieces in a medium bowl and set aside.

In a small saucepan, heat the heavy cream over medium heat until it starts to simmer. Do not boil.

Remove the saucepan from the heat and pour the hot cream over the chopped chocolate. Let it sit for 1-2 minutes to allow the chocolate to melt.

Add the unsalted butter, pure vanilla extract, and pinch of salt to the bowl and stir until the ingredients are well combined and the chocolate is completely melted.

If the ganache sauce is too thick, you can add a little bit of additional heavy cream, 1 tablespoon at a time, until it reaches the desired consistency.

Allow the ganache sauce to cool for a few minutes before serving.

Drizzle the chocolate ganache sauce over ice cream, cakes, brownies, or any other dessert of your choice.

Chocolate ganache sauce is a delicious and versatile sauce that can be used to add a rich and decadent touch to any dessert. Enjoy!

Salted Caramel Sauce:

Ingredients:

1 cup granulated sugar

6 tablespoons unsalted butter, at room temperature

1/2 cup heavy cream, at room temperature

1 teaspoon sea salt, or to taste

Instructions:

In a medium heavy-bottomed saucepan, heat the granulated sugar over medium heat, stirring constantly with a whisk or wooden spoon.

As the sugar melts, it will start to clump together, but keep stirring until it is completely melted and has turned into a deep amber color.

Add the butter to the melted sugar and stir until the butter is completely melted and well combined.

Slowly pour in the heavy cream, whisking constantly until the mixture is smooth and well combined.

Continue to cook the caramel sauce over medium heat, stirring constantly, for about 5 minutes, or until it thickens and coats the back of a spoon.

Remove the caramel sauce from the heat and stir in the sea salt to taste.

Let the salted caramel sauce cool for a few minutes before using it. It can be stored in an airtight container in the refrigerator for up to 2 weeks.

Salted caramel sauce is a delicious and versatile sauce that can be used as a topping for ice cream, cakes, pies, and many other desserts.

Raspberry Sauce

Ingredients:

2 cups fresh or frozen raspberries

1/2 cup granulated sugar

1 tablespoon freshly squeezed lemon juice

Instructions:

Rinse the raspberries under cold water and pat them dry with a paper towel. If you're using frozen raspberries, let them thaw at room temperature for about 10-15 minutes.

In a medium saucepan, combine the raspberries, sugar, and lemon juice.

Heat the mixture over medium-high heat, stirring occasionally, until the sugar has dissolved and the raspberries have broken down and released their juices. This should take about 5-7 minutes.

Reduce the heat to low and simmer the mixture for an additional 5-10 minutes, or until it has thickened slightly.

Remove the saucepan from the heat and let the mixture cool for a few minutes.

Pour the raspberry mixture through a fine-mesh sieve to remove the seeds and any lumps.

Use a rubber spatula to press the mixture through the sieve, if needed.

Discard the seeds and solids left in the sieve and transfer the raspberry sauce to a jar or container with a lid.

Cover the jar or container and refrigerate the raspberry sauce until it's completely chilled.

Once the raspberry sauce is chilled, it's ready to use! Drizzle it over your favorite desserts, like cheesecake or ice cream, or use it as a topping for pancakes or waffles. You can also mix it into cocktails

Lemon Curd Sauce

Ingredients:

1/2 cup freshly squeezed lemon juice

1/2 cup granulated sugar

3 large eggs

1/4 cup unsalted butter, cut into small pieces

Instructions:

In a medium-sized saucepan, whisk together the lemon juice, sugar, and eggs until smooth.

Place the saucepan over medium heat and cook, stirring constantly with a wooden spoon, until the mixture thickens and coats the back of the spoon. This should take about 8-10 minutes.

Remove the saucepan from the heat and add the butter. Stir until the butter is fully melted and incorporated into the sauce.

If the sauce is lumpy or not fully smooth, strain it through a fine-mesh strainer to remove any bits of cooked egg.

Let the lemon curd sauce cool to room temperature, then transfer it to an airtight container and refrigerate for at least 1 hour before serving.

To serve, spoon the lemon curd sauce over your favorite desserts such as cakes, cupcakes, scones or pastries.

Note: Lemon curd sauce can be stored in the refrigerator for up to 2 weeks.

Vanilla Custard Sauce

Ingredients:

2 cups whole milk

1/2 cup granulated sugar

4 large egg yolks

2 tablespoons cornstarch

1 teaspoon pure vanilla extract

Instructions:

In a medium-sized saucepan, heat the milk over medium heat until it just begins to simmer.

In a separate bowl, whisk together the sugar, egg yolks, and cornstarch until smooth and fully combined.

Slowly pour the heated milk into the egg mixture, whisking constantly to prevent the eggs from curdling.

Pour the mixture back into the saucepan and cook over medium heat, stirring constantly with a wooden spoon or spatula, until the custard thickens and coats the back of the spoon. This should take about 5-7 minutes.

Remove the saucepan from the heat and stir in the vanilla extract.

If the sauce is lumpy or not fully smooth, strain it through a fine-mesh strainer to remove any bits of cooked egg.

Let the custard sauce cool to room temperature, then transfer it to an airtight container and refrigerate for at least 1 hour before serving.

To serve, spoon the vanilla custard sauce over your favorite desserts such as pies, cakes, fruits, or pastries.

Note: Vanilla custard sauce can be stored in the refrigerator for up to 4 days.

Strawberry Sauce

Ingredients:

1 pound fresh or frozen strawberries

1/4 cup granulated sugar

2 tablespoons fresh lemon juice

Pinch of salt

Instructions:

If using fresh strawberries, remove the stems and cut them into small pieces. If using frozen strawberries, let them thaw and drain any excess liquid.

In a medium-sized saucepan, combine the strawberries, sugar, lemon juice, and salt.

Cook the mixture over medium heat, stirring occasionally, until the strawberries are soft and the sugar has fully dissolved. This should take about 10-12 minutes.

Use an immersion blender or transfer the mixture to a blender and blend until smooth.

If the sauce is too thick, you can add a tablespoon or two of water to thin it out.

Let the strawberry sauce cool to room temperature, then transfer it to an airtight container and refrigerate for at least 1 hour before serving.

To serve, spoon the strawberry sauce over your favorite desserts such as ice cream, cheesecake, pancakes or waffles.

Note: Strawberry sauce can be stored in the refrigerator for up to 1 week.

Soup

Vegetable Soup

Tomato Soup

Dill Tomato Soup

Lentil Soup

Chicken Noodle Soup

Butternut Squash Soup

Broccoli Cheddar Soup

Minestrone Soup

Gazpacho

Cream of Mushroom Soup

Chicken Tortilla Soup

Vegetable Soup:

Ingredients:

1 tablespoon olive oil

1 large onion, diced

3 cloves garlic, minced

2 carrots, peeled and sliced

2 stalks celery, sliced

1 sweet potato, peeled and chopped

1 zucchini, chopped

1 can (14 oz) diced tomatoes, with juice

6 cups vegetable stock

1 teaspoon dried thyme

1 teaspoon dried oregano

Salt and pepper, to taste

Fresh parsley, chopped (optional)

Instructions:

Heat the olive oil in a large soup pot over medium heat. Add the diced onion and sauté for 3-4 minutes, until softened.

Add the minced garlic and sauté for an additional minute.

Add the sliced carrots, celery, and sweet potato to the pot. Stir to combine and sauté for 5-7 minutes, until the vegetables begin to soften.

Add the chopped zucchini, diced tomatoes (with their juice), vegetable stock, dried thyme, and dried oregano to the pot. Stir to combine.

Bring the soup to a boil, then reduce the heat to low and let simmer for 20-30 minutes, or until all of the vegetables are tender.

Season with salt and pepper, to taste.

If desired, garnish with fresh chopped parsley before serving.

Classic and Comforting Tomato Soup:

Ingredients:

2 tablespoons olive oil

1 large onion, chopped

2 garlic cloves, minced

2 cans (28 oz) whole peeled tomatoes, with their juices

4 cups vegetable or chicken stock

1 teaspoon dried basil

1 teaspoon dried oregano

Salt and pepper, to taste

Optional: 1/2 cup heavy cream or coconut cream (for a vegan option)

Instructions:

Heat the olive oil in a large pot over medium heat. Add the chopped onion and sauté for 3-4 minutes, until softened.

Add the minced garlic and sauté for an additional minute.

Add the cans of whole peeled tomatoes, with their juices, to the pot. Use a wooden spoon to break up the tomatoes into smaller pieces.

Add the vegetable or chicken stock, dried basil, and dried oregano to the pot. Stir to combine.

Bring the soup to a boil, then reduce the heat to low and let simmer for 20-30 minutes, stirring occasionally.

Remove the pot from the heat and use an immersion blender or transfer the soup to a blender to puree until smooth.

Season with salt and pepper, to taste.

If desired, stir in 1/2 cup of heavy cream or coconut cream to add creaminess to the soup (omit for a vegan option).

Serve hot and enjoy your delicious and comforting tomato soup!

Note: For a gluten-free option, make sure to use gluten-free stock and check the ingredients on any canned tomatoes used.

Dill Tomato Soup

Ingredients:

2 tablespoons olive oil

1 large onion, chopped

3 cloves garlic, minced

2 cans (28 oz) diced tomatoes, with their juices

4 cups vegetable or chicken stock

1 teaspoon dried dill weed

1 teaspoon dried basil

Salt and pepper, to taste

Optional: 1/2 cup heavy cream or coconut cream (for a vegan option)

Instructions:

Heat the olive oil in a large pot over medium heat. Add the chopped onion and sauté for 3-4 minutes, until softened.

Add the minced garlic and sauté for an additional minute.

Add the cans of diced tomatoes, with their juices, to the pot. Stir to combine.

Add the vegetable or chicken stock, dried dill weed, and dried basil to the pot. Stir to combine.

Bring the soup to a boil, then reduce the heat to low and let simmer for 20-30 minutes, stirring occasionally.

Remove the pot from the heat and use an immersion blender or transfer the soup to a blender to puree until smooth.

Season with salt and pepper, to taste.

If desired, stir in 1/2 cup of heavy cream or coconut cream to add creaminess to the soup (omit for a vegan option).

Serve hot and enjoy your delicious and flavorful dill tomato soup!

Note: For a gluten-free option, make sure to use gluten-free stock and check the ingredients on any canned tomatoes used.

Delicious and Hearty Lentil Soup:

Ingredients:

2 tablespoons olive oil

1 large onion, chopped

3 cloves garlic, minced

2 carrots, peeled and chopped

2 celery stalks, chopped

1 teaspoon ground cumin

1 teaspoon ground coriander

1 teaspoon smoked paprika

1/2 teaspoon ground turmeric

1 cup dried green or brown lentils, rinsed and drained

4 cups vegetable stock

1 can (14 oz) diced tomatoes, with juice

Salt and pepper, to taste

Optional: Fresh parsley, chopped (for garnish)

Instructions:

Heat the olive oil in a large soup pot over medium heat. Add the chopped onion and sauté for 3-4 minutes, until softened.

Add the minced garlic and sauté for an additional minute.

Add the chopped carrots and celery to the pot. Stir to combine and sauté for 5-7 minutes, until the vegetables begin to soften.

Add the ground cumin, ground coriander, smoked paprika, and ground turmeric to the pot. Stir to combine.

Add the rinsed and drained lentils, vegetable stock, and diced tomatoes (with their juice) to the pot. Stir to combine.

Bring the soup to a boil, then reduce the heat to low and let simmer for 25-30 minutes, or until the lentils are tender.

Season with salt and pepper, to taste.

If desired, garnish with fresh chopped parsley before serving.

Comforting and Delicious Chicken Noodle Soup:

Ingredients:

2 tablespoons olive oil

1 onion, chopped

3 cloves garlic, minced

2 carrots, peeled and chopped

2 celery stalks, chopped

1 teaspoon dried thyme

1 bay leaf

8 cups chicken stock

2 cups cooked and shredded chicken

2 cups uncooked gluten-free egg noodles (or regular egg noodles if not gluten-free)

Salt and pepper, to taste

Optional: Fresh parsley, chopped (for garnish)

Instructions:

Heat the olive oil in a large pot over medium heat. Add the chopped onion and sauté for 3-4 minutes, until softened.

Add the minced garlic and sauté for an additional minute.

Add the chopped carrots and celery to the pot. Stir to combine and sauté for 5-7 minutes, until the vegetables begin to soften.

Add the dried thyme and bay leaf to the pot. Stir to combine.

Pour the chicken stock into the pot and bring to a boil.

Add the uncooked gluten-free egg noodles (or regular egg noodles if not gluten-free) and let simmer for 10-12 minutes, until the noodles are tender.

Add the cooked and shredded chicken to the pot. Stir to combine and let simmer for an additional 5-10 minutes, until the chicken is heated through.

Season with salt and pepper, to taste.

If desired, garnish with fresh chopped parsley before serving.

Butternut Squash Soup:

Ingredients:

1 medium butternut squash, peeled and cubed

1 medium onion, diced

2 cloves garlic, minced

2 cups vegetable broth

1 cup coconut milk (or heavy cream if not vegan)

2 tablespoons olive oil

Salt and pepper, to taste

Instructions:

In a large pot, heat olive oil over medium-high heat. Add diced onion and minced garlic and sauté until the onion is soft and translucent, about 5 minutes.

Add the butternut squash to the pot and sauté for another 5-7 minutes, until the squash starts to brown.

Pour in the vegetable broth and bring to a boil. Reduce heat and let simmer until the squash is tender, about 20-25 minutes.

Use an immersion blender (or transfer the soup to a blender) and blend until smooth.

Stir in coconut milk (or heavy cream) and season with salt and pepper to taste.

Heat the soup until warm and serve hot with crusty bread or crackers on the side.

Enjoy your delicious and healthy Butternut Squash Soup!

Broccoli Cheddar Soup:

Ingredients:

4 cups broccoli florets

1/4 cup unsalted butter

1/4 cup gluten-free flour

2 cups milk

2 cups vegetable or chicken broth

1/2 teaspoon garlic powder

1/2 teaspoon onion powder

1/4 teaspoon paprika

1/4 teaspoon salt

1/4 teaspoon black pepper

2 cups shredded cheddar cheese

Croutons or crusty bread, for serving (optional)

Instructions:

Steam the broccoli florets until tender, then set aside.

In a large pot, melt the butter over medium heat. Add the gluten-free flour and stir to make a roux. Cook, stirring constantly, for 2-3 minutes.

Gradually whisk in the milk, then the vegetable or chicken broth. Add the garlic powder, onion powder, paprika, salt, and black pepper.

Bring the soup to a boil, stirring constantly, then reduce the heat and let simmer for 10 minutes.

Add the steamed broccoli and stir to combine.

Remove the pot from the heat and stir in the shredded cheddar cheese until melted and smooth.

Serve hot with croutons or crusty bread on top (optional).

Enjoy your delicious and gluten-free Broccoli Cheddar Soup!

Minestrone Soup:

Ingredients:

1 tablespoon olive oil

1 onion, diced

3 cloves garlic, minced

2 carrots, diced

2 celery stalks, diced

1 zucchini, diced

1 yellow squash, diced

1 can (15 oz) diced tomatoes

4 cups vegetable broth

1 can (15 oz) kidney beans, drained and rinsed

1 cup gluten-free pasta (such as elbow or fusilli)

1 teaspoon dried basil

1/2 teaspoon dried oregano

Salt and pepper, to taste

Instructions:

In a large pot, heat olive oil over medium-high heat. Add diced onion and minced garlic and sauté until the onion is soft and translucent, about 5 minutes.

Add diced carrots, celery, zucchini, and yellow squash to the pot and sauté for another 5-7 minutes, until the vegetables are slightly softened.

Add diced tomatoes, vegetable broth, and drained kidney beans to the pot. Stir to combine.

Bring the soup to a boil, then reduce heat to a simmer and let cook for 10 minutes.

Add gluten-free pasta, dried basil, and dried oregano to the pot. Stir to combine and cook for an additional 10-12 minutes, until the pasta is tender.

Season with salt and pepper to taste.

Serve hot and enjoy your delicious and healthy Minestrone Soup!

You can also add some fresh herbs or grated Parmesan cheese on top of the soup to enhance its flavors.

Gazpacho:

Ingredients:

4 large ripe tomatoes, roughly chopped

1 large cucumber, peeled and roughly chopped

1 red bell pepper, seeded and roughly chopped

1 green bell pepper, seeded and roughly chopped

1 small red onion, roughly chopped

2 garlic cloves, minced

1/4 cup red wine vinegar

1/4 cup olive oil

1/4 cup cold water

Salt and pepper, to taste

Optional toppings: chopped fresh herbs (such as basil or cilantro), diced avocado, croutons, or a drizzle of olive oil

Instructions:

In a blender or food processor, combine chopped tomatoes, cucumber, red and green bell peppers, red onion, and minced garlic. Pulse until vegetables are coarsely pureed.

Add red wine vinegar, olive oil, and cold water to the blender. Pulse again until well combined.

Season the gazpacho with salt and pepper to taste. If the soup is too thick, add more water as needed to thin it out.

Chill the gazpacho in the refrigerator for at least 30 minutes or until ready to serve.

When ready to serve, stir the soup and divide it into bowls. Garnish with chopped fresh herbs, diced avocado, croutons, or a drizzle of olive oil if desired.

Enjoy your refreshing and delicious Gazpacho! You can also adjust the recipe by adding or omitting ingredients to suit your taste preferences.

Cream of Mushroom Soup:

Ingredients:

2 tablespoons olive oil or vegan butter

1 onion, chopped

2 cloves garlic, minced

16 oz mushrooms, sliced

1 teaspoon dried thyme

1 teaspoon dried rosemary

4 cups vegetable broth

1/2 cup coconut milk or cashew cream

Salt and pepper, to taste

Optional: chopped fresh herbs for garnish

Instructions:

In a large pot, heat the olive oil or vegan butter over medium-high heat. Add the chopped onion and minced garlic and sauté until the onion is soft and translucent, about 5 minutes.

Add the sliced mushrooms, dried thyme, and dried rosemary to the pot. Sauté for another 5-7 minutes, until the mushrooms are softened.

Add the vegetable broth to the pot and bring the mixture to a boil. Reduce the heat and let simmer for 10-15 minutes, until the mushrooms are very tender.

Use an immersion blender or transfer the mixture to a blender or food processor and blend until smooth.

Return the soup to the pot and stir in the coconut milk or cashew cream. Simmer for another 5-10 minutes until heated through.

Season with salt and pepper to taste.

Serve hot and garnish with chopped fresh herbs, if desired.

Enjoy your creamy and delicious Cream of Mushroom Soup, which is also vegan and gluten-free!

Chicken Tortilla Soup:

Ingredients:

2 tablespoons olive oil

1 onion, chopped

3 cloves garlic, minced

1 jalapeño pepper, seeded and chopped

1 red bell pepper, chopped

1 green bell pepper, chopped

1 teaspoon ground cumin

1 teaspoon smoked paprika

1/2 teaspoon chili powder

6 cups chicken broth

1 can (14 oz) diced tomatoes, undrained

1 can (14 oz) black beans, drained and rinsed

2 cups shredded cooked chicken

Salt and pepper, to taste

Optional toppings: shredded cheese, chopped fresh cilantro, sour cream, diced avocado, tortilla strips or chips

Instructions:

In a large pot, heat the olive oil over medium-high heat. Add the chopped onion, minced garlic, chopped jalapeño pepper, and chopped red and green bell peppers. Sauté until the vegetables are softened, about 5 minutes.

Add the ground cumin, smoked paprika, and chili powder to the pot. Sauté for another 1-2 minutes, until the spices are fragrant.

Add the chicken broth, diced tomatoes (undrained), and black beans to the pot. Bring the mixture to a boil, then reduce the heat and let simmer for 10-15 minutes.

Add the shredded cooked chicken to the pot and simmer for another 5-10 minutes until heated through.

Season the soup with salt and pepper to taste.

Serve hot and garnish with shredded cheese, chopped fresh cilantro, sour cream, diced avocado, and tortilla strips or chips, if desired.

Enjoy your spicy and flavorful Chicken Tortilla Soup, which can also be made gluten-free by skipping the tortilla strips or using gluten-free tortilla chips!

Poultry

When dealing with stomach issues my family has learned that poultry is main dish to not only prepare but also digest. All of these recipes have been developed over the last six years and were made with digestive problems in mind.

Chicken Wraps

1 package of Chicken tenderloins

12oz bacon

Shredded lettuce

Mozzarella cheese

1 package of tortillas or find the recipe in bread

Paprika

Bbq seasoning

BBq sauce (find the recipe in sauces)

½ c Mayo

Preheat oven to 350 degrees

On a sheet tray place chicken tenderloins. Sprinkle with seasoning. Bake for 15 min.

Cook bacon until crisp. Let cool then crumble. Add mayo and mix. Set in fridge until ready to use.

On the stove heat BBQ sauce until liquid.

Dredge Chicken in BBQ sauce then cook for another 5 min. Repeat until chicken is done.

On tortilla shells spread mayo mixture. Add lettuce and cheese. Place Chicken on top then roll up folding the bottom up but leave the top open.

Great paired with fries, tots or rice.

Bruschetta Stuffed Chicken

Directions can be found on my YouTube channel

Plumb Sauce (recipe is in sauces)

1Tbsp Salt

1 Tbsp Pepper

1 Cup Brown sugar

3 Romain Tomatoes

1 small red onion

1 Bushel fresh parsley

Boneless, Skinless chicken thighs

1 Garlic Clove

Mix salt, pepper and brown sugar together in a small mixing bowl. Drudge chicken in the mixture. Be sure to coat both sides. Set in lightly greased baking pan.

In a food pressor chop tomato, onion, peeled garlic clove and a few sprigs of parsley. Fresh Basile can also be added.

Fill the inside of the chicken thighs with Bruschetta. Cover with remaining brown sugar mix. Bake at 350 degrees for 30 min. Check to make sure it done before serving.

Drizzle the plumb sauce over the cut chicken and serve.

Pair with pasta and garlic bread.

Splenda brown sugar mixture can be instead of traditional brown sugar

Grilled Lemon Garlic Chicken:

Ingredients:

4 boneless, skinless chicken breasts

1/4 cup fresh lemon juice

2 cloves garlic, minced

2 tablespoons chopped fresh herbs (such as parsley, thyme, or rosemary)

1/4 teaspoon salt

1/4 teaspoon black pepper

2 tablespoons olive oil

Instructions:

In a large bowl, whisk together the lemon juice, garlic, herbs, salt, and pepper. Slowly pour in the olive oil while whisking to create a smooth marinade.

Add the chicken breasts to the bowl and turn them to coat them evenly with the marinade. Cover the bowl with plastic wrap and marinate in the refrigerator for at least 30 minutes or up to 4 hours.

Preheat a grill to medium-high heat.

Remove the chicken from the marinade and discard any excess marinade. Grill the chicken for 6-7 minutes per side, or until the internal temperature reaches 165°F (74°C).

Remove the chicken from the grill and let it rest for 5 minutes before serving.

Chicken Curry:

Ingredients:

1 1/2 lbs boneless, skinless chicken breasts, cut into bite-sized pieces

1 tablespoon olive oil

1 onion, chopped

2 cloves garlic, minced

1 tablespoon grated fresh ginger

2 tablespoons curry powder

1 teaspoon ground cumin

1 teaspoon ground coriander

1/2 teaspoon ground turmeric

1/4 teaspoon cayenne pepper (optional)

1 can (13.5 oz) coconut milk

1 cup chicken broth

Salt and pepper, to taste

Fresh cilantro, chopped (for garnish)

Cooked rice or cauliflower rice (for serving)

Instructions:

Heat the olive oil in a large skillet or Dutch oven over medium-high heat. Add the chicken and cook until browned on all sides, about 5 minutes. Remove the chicken from the skillet and set it aside on a plate.

Add the chopped onion to the skillet and cook until softened, about 3 minutes. Add the garlic and ginger and cook for 1 minute, stirring constantly.

Add the curry powder, cumin, coriander, turmeric, and cayenne pepper (if using) to the skillet and stir to coat the onion mixture. Cook for 1-2 minutes, stirring constantly, until fragrant.

Pour in the coconut milk and chicken broth and stir to combine. Bring the mixture to a simmer.

Add the browned chicken back to the skillet and stir to coat it with the curry sauce. Cover the skillet and let the curry simmer for 20-25 minutes, stirring occasionally, until the chicken is cooked through and tender.

Season the curry with salt and pepper, to taste. Serve the curry over cooked rice or cauliflower rice and garnish with chopped cilantro.

Baked Chicken Thighs: Season chicken thighs with herbs such as thyme and rosemary, and bake in the oven until crispy. This can be made gluten-free and dairy-free.

Chicken Fajitas:

Ingredients:

1 lb boneless, skinless chicken breasts, sliced into thin strips

1 tablespoon olive oil

1 onion, sliced

1 bell pepper, sliced

1 teaspoon chili powder

1/2 teaspoon ground cumin

1/2 teaspoon paprika

1/4 teaspoon garlic powder

Salt and pepper, to taste

Gluten-free tortillas

Sliced avocado, for serving (optional)

Salsa, for serving (optional)

Dairy-free sour cream or cheese, for serving (optional)

Instructions:

Heat the olive oil in a large skillet over medium-high heat. Add the sliced chicken and cook until browned on all sides and cooked through, about 5-7 minutes. Remove the chicken from the skillet and set it aside on a plate.

Add the sliced onion and bell pepper to the skillet and cook for 3-4 minutes, until softened.

Add the chili powder, cumin, paprika, garlic powder, salt, and pepper to the skillet and stir to coat the onion and pepper mixture. Cook for 1-2 minutes, stirring constantly, until fragrant.

Return the cooked chicken to the skillet and stir to combine with the onion and pepper mixture. Cook for 1-2 minutes, until heated through.

Serve the chicken fajitas with gluten-free tortillas, sliced avocado, salsa, and dairy-free sour cream or cheese, if desired.

Chicken Stir Fry:

Ingredients:

1 lb boneless, skinless chicken breasts, cut into bite-sized pieces

2 tablespoons olive oil, divided

1/2 cup broccoli florets

1/2 cup sliced carrots

1/2 cup sliced bell peppers

1/2 onion, sliced

2 cloves garlic, minced

1 tablespoon grated fresh ginger

1 tablespoon gluten-free soy sauce or tamari

1 tablespoon rice vinegar

1 teaspoon honey

1/4 teaspoon red pepper flakes (optional)

Salt and pepper, to taste

Gluten-free rice noodles or cauliflower rice, for serving

Instructions:

Heat 1 tablespoon of the olive oil in a large skillet or wok over high heat. Add the chicken and cook until browned on all sides and cooked through, about 5-7 minutes. Remove the chicken from the skillet and set it aside on a plate.

Add the remaining tablespoon of olive oil to the skillet. Add the broccoli, carrots, bell peppers, onion, garlic, and ginger to the skillet and stir-fry for 3-4 minutes, until the vegetables are tender-crisp.

In a small bowl, whisk together the gluten-free soy sauce or tamari, rice vinegar, honey, red pepper flakes (if using), salt, and pepper.

Return the cooked chicken to the skillet and pour the soy sauce mixture over everything. Stir-fry for 1-2 minutes, until the chicken and vegetables are coated in the sauce and everything is heated through.

Serve the chicken stir-fry over cooked gluten-free rice noodles or cauliflower rice.

Grilled Chicken Caesar Salad:

Ingredients:

1 lb boneless, skinless chicken breasts

1 tablespoon olive oil

Salt and pepper, to taste

1 head of romaine lettuce, chopped

Gluten-free croutons

Dairy-free Caesar dressing (recipe below)

For the Dairy-Free Caesar Dressing:

1/2 cup raw cashews, soaked in water for 2 hours or overnight

2 tablespoons fresh lemon juice

1 tablespoon Dijon mustard

1 tablespoon capers

1 clove garlic, minced

1/4 teaspoon salt

1/4 teaspoon pepper

1/2 cup water

1/4 cup extra-virgin olive oil

Instructions:

Preheat a grill to medium-high heat. Brush the chicken breasts with olive oil and season with salt and pepper.

Grill the chicken for 6-8 minutes per side, until cooked through and no longer pink in the middle. Remove the chicken from the grill and let it rest for 5 minutes before slicing it into strips.

While the chicken is grilling, make the Dairy-Free Caesar Dressing. Drain and rinse the soaked cashews and add them to a blender or food processor. Add the lemon juice, Dijon mustard, capers, garlic, salt, and pepper, and blend until smooth.

With the blender or food processor running, slowly pour in the water and olive oil, and blend until the dressing is creamy and emulsified.

Assemble the salad by arranging the chopped romaine lettuce on a platter or in individual bowls. Top with the sliced grilled chicken, gluten-free croutons, and a generous drizzle of the Dairy-Free Caesar Dressing.

Enjoy your delicious and healthy Grilled Chicken Caesar Salad, made gluten-free and dairy-free!

Chicken Parmesan:

Ingredients:

4 boneless, skinless chicken breasts

1/2 cup gluten-free breadcrumbs

1/2 cup grated Parmesan cheese

1 teaspoon garlic powder

1 teaspoon dried basil

1/2 teaspoon salt

1/4 teaspoon black pepper

2 eggs, beaten

Gluten-free pasta, for serving

Dairy-free cheese, for serving

Instructions:

Preheat the oven to 400°F (200°C). Line a baking sheet with parchment paper.

In a shallow dish, combine the gluten-free breadcrumbs, grated Parmesan cheese, garlic powder, dried basil, salt, and black pepper.

In another shallow dish, beat the eggs.

Dip each chicken breast in the beaten eggs, then coat it in the breadcrumb mixture, pressing the breadcrumbs and cheese onto the chicken to ensure they stick.

Place the breaded chicken breasts on the prepared baking sheet and bake for 25-30 minutes, until the chicken is cooked through and the coating is golden and crispy.

While the chicken is baking, cook the gluten-free pasta according to the package instructions.

Once the chicken is done, remove it from the oven and let it cool for a few minutes before slicing it into strips.

Serve the sliced Chicken Parmesan over the cooked gluten-free pasta, and top with dairy-free cheese.

Enjoy your delicious and healthy Chicken Parmesan, made gluten-free and dairy-free!

Chicken and Rice Soup:

Ingredients:

1 tablespoon olive oil

1 onion, diced

2 carrots, peeled and diced

2 celery stalks, diced

2 cloves garlic, minced

1 teaspoon dried thyme

1 bay leaf

8 cups chicken broth (make sure it's gluten-free)

1 cup uncooked white or brown rice

2 cups cooked and shredded chicken (you can use leftover chicken or cook it specifically for the soup)

Salt and pepper, to taste

Gluten-free crackers or bread, for serving

Instructions:

Heat the olive oil in a large pot over medium heat. Add the onion, carrots, and celery, and cook until the vegetables are soft and the onion is translucent, about 5-7 minutes.

Add the garlic, dried thyme, and bay leaf, and cook for another minute, until fragrant.

Add the chicken broth to the pot and bring to a boil. Add the uncooked rice and reduce the heat to low. Cover the pot and let the soup simmer for 15-20 minutes, until the rice is cooked and tender.

Add the shredded chicken to the pot and let it warm up in the soup for a few minutes. Season the soup with salt and pepper to taste.

Remove the bay leaf from the pot and discard.

Serve the Chicken and Rice Soup hot, with gluten-free crackers or bread on the side.

Teriyaki Chicken:

Ingredients:

4 boneless, skinless chicken breasts

1 cup gluten-free teriyaki sauce (homemade or store-bought)

2 tablespoons olive oil

Salt and pepper, to taste

Optional toppings: sesame seeds, sliced green onions

Instructions:

In a large bowl, whisk together the gluten-free teriyaki sauce and olive oil.

Add the chicken breasts to the bowl and toss them in the marinade to coat them evenly. Cover the bowl with plastic wrap and refrigerate for at least 30 minutes, or up to 2 hours.

Preheat the grill to medium-high heat or preheat the oven to 400°F (200°C).

Remove the chicken breasts from the marinade and discard any excess marinade.

Season the chicken breasts with salt and pepper, to taste.

If grilling, place the chicken breasts on the grill and cook for 5-6 minutes per side, or until cooked through and no longer pink in the center. If baking, place the chicken breasts on a baking sheet and bake for 20-25 minutes, or until cooked through and no longer pink in the center.

Once the chicken is done, remove it from the grill or oven and let it rest for a few minutes before slicing it into strips.

Serve the sliced Teriyaki Chicken hot, garnished with sesame seeds and sliced green onions if desired.

Chicken Piccata:

Ingredients:

4 boneless, skinless chicken breasts

Salt and pepper, to taste

1/2 cup gluten-free all-purpose flour

2 tablespoons olive oil

2 tablespoons dairy-free butter

1/4 cup fresh lemon juice

1/4 cup gluten-free chicken broth

2 tablespoons capers

Fresh parsley, chopped, for garnish

Instructions:

Season the chicken breasts with salt and pepper on both sides.

Place the gluten-free all-purpose flour in a shallow dish.

Coat each chicken breast in the flour, shaking off any excess.

Heat the olive oil in a large skillet over medium-high heat.

Add the chicken breasts to the skillet and cook for 4-5 minutes per side, or until golden brown and cooked through.

Once the chicken is cooked, remove it from the skillet and set it aside on a plate.

In the same skillet, add the dairy-free butter, lemon juice, gluten-free chicken broth, and capers. Whisk everything together and let the sauce simmer for 2-3 minutes, or until slightly thickened.

Return the chicken to the skillet and coat it in the sauce. Cook for an additional minute or two, until the chicken is heated through and fully coated in the sauce.

Serve the Chicken Piccata hot, garnished with fresh parsley.

Chicken Tacos:

Ingredients:

4 boneless, skinless chicken breasts

2 tablespoons olive oil

2 teaspoons ground cumin

2 teaspoons chili powder

1/2 teaspoon garlic powder

Salt and pepper, to taste

8-10 gluten-free taco shells

Dairy-free toppings, such as salsa, guacamole, diced tomatoes, shredded lettuce, and dairy-free cheese

Instructions:

Preheat the oven to 375°F (190°C).

Heat the olive oil in a large skillet over medium-high heat.

Season the chicken breasts with the ground cumin, chili powder, garlic powder, salt, and pepper.

Add the chicken breasts to the skillet and cook for 5-6 minutes per side, or until cooked through and no longer pink in the center.

Once the chicken is cooked, remove it from the skillet and let it rest for a few minutes before slicing it into strips.

Warm the gluten-free taco shells in the preheated oven for 5-6 minutes.

Fill each taco shell with the sliced chicken, and top with your favorite dairy-free toppings such as salsa, guacamole, diced tomatoes, shredded lettuce, and dairy-free cheese.

Serve the Chicken Tacos hot and enjoy!

Chicken Alfredo:

Ingredients:

2 boneless, skinless chicken breasts

8 ounces gluten-free pasta

2 tablespoons olive oil

2 cloves garlic, minced

1/2 cup full-fat coconut milk

1/4 cup nutritional yeast

Salt and pepper, to taste

Instructions:

Cook the gluten-free pasta according to package instructions. Drain and set aside.

Heat the olive oil in a large skillet over medium-high heat.

Season the chicken breasts with salt and pepper, and cook in the skillet for 6-8 minutes per side, or until cooked through and no longer pink in the center.

Once the chicken is cooked, remove it from the skillet and let it rest for a few minutes before slicing it into strips.

In the same skillet, add the minced garlic and sauté for 1-2 minutes, or until fragrant.

Add the coconut milk and nutritional yeast to the skillet, and stir to combine. Simmer for 2-3 minutes, or until the sauce has thickened.

Add the cooked gluten-free pasta and sliced chicken to the skillet, and toss to coat with the Alfredo sauce.

Serve the Chicken Alfredo hot, and enjoy!

Roasted Chicken with Vegetables:

Ingredients:

1 whole chicken (4-5 pounds)

2-3 cups of mixed vegetables (such as carrots, potatoes, onions, and bell peppers), cut into chunks

2 tablespoons olive oil

Salt and pepper, to taste

Optional herbs and spices, such as garlic powder, dried thyme, or rosemary

Instructions:

Preheat the oven to 375°F.

Rinse the chicken under cold water and pat dry with paper towels.

Season the chicken inside and out with salt, pepper, and any other herbs and spices you prefer.

Place the chicken breast-side up in a roasting pan or large baking dish.

Toss the vegetables in olive oil and season with salt and pepper.

Arrange the vegetables around the chicken in the roasting pan.

Roast the chicken and vegetables in the preheated oven for 1 1/2 to 2 hours, or until the chicken is cooked through and the juices run clear when you pierce the thigh with a knife.

Let the chicken rest for 10 minutes before carving and serving with the roasted vegetables.

Optional step: If you want the chicken to have a crispy skin, you can increase the oven temperature to 425°F for the last 10-15 minutes of cooking time. Keep an eye on the chicken to make sure it doesn't burn.

Chicken Shawarma:

Ingredients:

2 pounds boneless, skinless chicken thighs or breasts

2 tablespoons olive oil

2 tablespoons lemon juice

1 tablespoon paprika

1 tablespoon cumin

1 teaspoon turmeric

1/2 teaspoon cinnamon

1/2 teaspoon garlic powder

Salt and pepper, to taste

Gluten-free pita bread, for serving

Dairy-free toppings such as hummus, tahini, chopped lettuce, sliced tomatoes, and pickles

Instructions:

In a large bowl, whisk together the olive oil, lemon juice, paprika, cumin, turmeric, cinnamon, garlic powder, salt, and pepper.

Add the chicken to the bowl and toss to coat with the marinade.

Cover the bowl with plastic wrap and marinate in the refrigerator for at least 30 minutes, or up to 24 hours.

Preheat a grill or grill pan to medium-high heat.

Remove the chicken from the marinade and discard any excess marinade.

Grill the chicken for 5-7 minutes per side, or until cooked through and no longer pink in the center.

Let the chicken rest for a few minutes before slicing into thin strips.

Serve the chicken in gluten-free pita bread with dairy-free toppings such as hummus, tahini, chopped lettuce, sliced tomatoes, and pickles.

Optional step: For extra flavor, you can add sliced onions and peppers to the grill to cook alongside the chicken.

Chicken Satay:

Ingredients:

1 lb chicken breast, cut into thin strips

1 cup coconut milk

2 tablespoons soy sauce (gluten-free, if desired)

1 tablespoon fish sauce

2 tablespoons brown sugar

2 tablespoons vegetable oil

2 cloves garlic, minced

1 tablespoon fresh lemongrass, minced

1 tablespoon fresh ginger, grated

1/4 teaspoon turmeric

Salt and pepper to taste

Wooden skewers, soaked in water for at least 30 minutes

For the Peanut Sauce:

1/2 cup creamy peanut butter

1/4 cup coconut milk

2 tablespoons soy sauce (gluten-free, if desired)

2 tablespoons brown sugar

1 tablespoon lime juice

1 teaspoon Sriracha or other hot sauce (optional)

Instructions:

In a large bowl, whisk together coconut milk, soy sauce, fish sauce, brown sugar, vegetable oil, garlic, lemongrass, ginger, turmeric, salt, and pepper. Add the chicken strips and toss to coat. Cover the bowl with plastic wrap and refrigerate for at least 2 hours, or overnight.

Preheat grill to medium-high heat or preheat oven to 375°F.

Thread the chicken strips onto the wooden skewers. If grilling, place the skewers on the grill and cook for about 5-6 minutes on each side or until cooked through. If baking, place the skewers on a baking sheet lined with parchment paper and bake for about 20-25 minutes or until cooked through.

While the chicken is cooking, prepare the peanut sauce. In a small saucepan over medium heat, whisk together peanut butter, coconut milk, soy sauce, brown sugar, lime juice, and Sriracha (if using). Cook for 2-3 minutes, stirring constantly, until the sauce is smooth and heated through.

Serve the chicken satay with the peanut sauce on the side for dipping.

Chicken Cordon Bleu:

Ingredients:

4 boneless, skinless chicken breasts

8 thin slices of ham

4 slices of Swiss cheese

1/2 cup all-purpose flour

2 eggs

1 cup panko breadcrumbs

Salt and pepper

Vegetable oil, for frying

1/2 cup dry white wine

2 shallots, finely chopped

1/2 cup heavy cream

2 tablespoons unsalted butter

Instructions:

Preheat your oven to 375°F.

Lay each chicken breast flat on a cutting board and use a meat mallet to pound them out to an even thickness of about 1/4 inch.

Season both sides of each chicken breast with salt and pepper.

Place 2 slices of ham on each chicken breast, followed by 1 slice of Swiss cheese.

Roll up each chicken breast tightly, tucking in the ends to prevent the filling from falling out.

Set up three shallow bowls: one with flour, one with beaten eggs, and one with panko breadcrumbs.

Dredge each chicken breast in the flour, shaking off any excess.

Dip each chicken breast in the beaten eggs, then coat thoroughly in the panko breadcrumbs, pressing lightly to ensure the crumbs adhere.

Heat about 1/4 inch of vegetable oil in a large skillet over medium-high heat. Once the oil is hot, add the chicken breasts and cook until golden brown on all sides, about 4-5 minutes per side.

Transfer the chicken breasts to a baking sheet and bake in the preheated oven for 15-20 minutes, until cooked through and the cheese is melted and bubbly.

Meanwhile, prepare the sauce. In a small saucepan, melt the butter over medium heat. Add the shallots and cook until soft and translucent, about 2-3 minutes.

Add the white wine to the pan and bring to a simmer. Cook until the wine has reduced by half, about 5 minutes.

Stir in the heavy cream and continue cooking until the sauce has thickened slightly, about 5-7 minutes.

Serve the chicken Cordon Bleu hot, with the creamy white wine sauce spooned over the top. Enjoy!

Duck Confit:

Ingredients:

4 duck legs

2 cups duck fat (or enough to cover the duck legs)

1 tablespoon kosher salt

1 teaspoon black pepper

4 cloves garlic, minced

2 sprigs fresh thyme

2 bay leaves

1 tablespoon olive oil

2 cups mixed root vegetables (such as carrots, parsnips, and turnips), peeled and chopped into bite-sized pieces

Salt and pepper, to taste

Instructions:

Preheat your oven to 300°F.

Season the duck legs with kosher salt and black pepper.

In a small saucepan, melt the duck fat over low heat until it is liquid.

In a baking dish or Dutch oven, place the duck legs in a single layer. Add the minced garlic, thyme, and bay leaves.

Pour the melted duck fat over the duck legs, making sure they are fully submerged.

Cover the baking dish or Dutch oven tightly with aluminum foil or a lid.

Transfer the dish to the oven and bake for 2-3 hours, or until the duck is tender and falls off the bone.

Remove the duck legs from the fat and let them cool slightly.

In a separate skillet, heat the olive oil over medium-high heat. Add the chopped root vegetables and cook until they are browned and tender, about 10-12 minutes.

Season the vegetables with salt and pepper to taste.

To serve, place a duck leg on each plate and spoon some of the roasted root vegetables alongside. Serve immediately and enjoy your delicious Duck Confit!

Coq au Vin:

Ingredients:

4-6 chicken thighs or legs

Salt and pepper

4 slices bacon, diced

1 onion, chopped

3 cloves garlic, minced

2 cups mushrooms, sliced

1 1/2 cups red wine

1 1/2 cups chicken broth

2 tablespoons tomato paste

2 bay leaves

1 teaspoon dried thyme

1 tablespoon butter

1 tablespoon all-purpose flour

1 cup frozen pearl onions

Chopped parsley, for garnish

Instructions:

Preheat your oven to 350°F.

Season the chicken with salt and pepper.

In a large Dutch oven or heavy-bottomed pot, cook the bacon over medium heat until crispy. Remove with a slotted spoon and set aside.

Add the chicken to the pot and cook until browned on both sides, about 6-8 minutes per side. Remove the chicken and set aside.

Add the onion, garlic, and mushrooms to the pot and sauté until the vegetables are softened and the mushrooms are browned, about 6-8 minutes.

Add the red wine, chicken broth, tomato paste, bay leaves, and thyme to the pot. Bring the mixture to a simmer.

Return the chicken and bacon to the pot and cover with a lid.

Transfer the pot to the oven and cook for 1 1/2 to 2 hours, or until the chicken is cooked through and tender.

In a small skillet, melt the butter over medium heat. Add the flour and whisk until smooth. Cook the roux for 2-3 minutes, or until lightly browned.

Add the roux to the pot and stir to thicken the sauce.

In a separate skillet, sauté the pearl onions until they are browned and caramelized.

Add the pearl onions to the pot and stir to combine.

Garnish with chopped parsley and serve hot with crusty bread or over a bed of mashed potatoes. Enjoy your delicious Coq au Vin!

Chicken Marsala:

Ingredients:

4 boneless, skinless chicken breasts

Salt and pepper

1/2 cup all-purpose flour

4 tablespoons unsalted butter

2 tablespoons olive oil

8 oz mushrooms, sliced

2 shallots, minced

2 cloves garlic, minced

1/2 cup Marsala wine

1/2 cup chicken broth

1/2 cup heavy cream

Chopped fresh parsley, for garnish

Instructions:

Preheat your oven to 200°F.

Season the chicken breasts with salt and pepper.

Dredge the chicken breasts in the flour, shaking off any excess.

In a large skillet, melt 2 tablespoons of butter with 1 tablespoon of olive oil over medium-high heat.

Once the butter is melted and bubbly, add the chicken breasts to the skillet and cook until browned on both sides, about 4-5 minutes per side. Remove the chicken from the skillet and place it in the oven to keep warm.

Add the remaining butter and olive oil to the skillet. Once melted, add the mushrooms and shallots to the skillet and sauté for 3-4 minutes, or until the mushrooms are browned and the shallots are softened.

Add the minced garlic to the skillet and sauté for an additional minute.

Pour in the Marsala wine and chicken broth and bring the mixture to a simmer. Scrape any browned bits from the bottom of the skillet to incorporate them into the sauce.

Simmer the sauce for 10-12 minutes, or until it has reduced and thickened slightly.

Stir in the heavy cream and simmer for an additional 2-3 minutes.

Add the chicken breasts back to the skillet, spooning the sauce over them to coat.

Garnish with chopped fresh parsley and serve hot with a side of pasta, rice, or roasted vegetables. Enjoy your delicious Chicken Marsala!

Turkey Roulade:

Ingredients:

1 (3-4 lb) boneless, skinless turkey breast

Salt and pepper

1 cup fresh parsley leaves, chopped

1/2 cup walnuts, chopped

1/2 cup dried cranberries, chopped

2 tablespoons fresh rosemary, chopped

2 tablespoons fresh thyme, chopped

3 tablespoons olive oil

3 cloves garlic, minced

1/2 cup chicken broth

Kitchen twine

Instructions:

Preheat your oven to 375°F.

Butterfly the turkey breast by cutting it in half lengthwise, stopping 1/2 inch from the edge so that it opens like a book.

Pound the turkey breast with a meat mallet until it is even in thickness.

Season the turkey breast with salt and pepper on both sides.

In a mixing bowl, combine the chopped parsley, walnuts, dried cranberries, rosemary, thyme, olive oil, and minced garlic. Mix until well combined.

Spread the filling evenly over the turkey breast.

Starting at one end, roll up the turkey breast tightly, tucking in the edges to create a compact roll.

Tie the turkey roll with kitchen twine at 1-inch intervals to secure it.

Place the turkey roll in a roasting pan and pour the chicken broth into the pan.

Roast the turkey for 1 to 1 1/2 hours, or until the internal temperature of the turkey reaches 165°F.

Remove the turkey from the oven and let it rest for 10-15 minutes before slicing.

Slice the turkey roulade into 1/2-inch thick slices and serve hot with a side of roasted vegetables or cranberry sauce. Enjoy your delicious Turkey Roulade!

Beef

Beef Stroganoff

Beef Bourguignon

Beef and Mushroom Meatloaf

Beef Goulash

Beef and Potato Casserole

Spaghetti Bolognese

Beef Brisket

Philly Cheesesteak

Beef Shawarma

Mongolian Beef

Corned Beef and Cabbage

Beef Wellington

Steak Diane

Beef Carpaccio

Braised Short Ribs

Prime Rib Roast

Beef Stroganoff

Ingredients:

1 pound beef sirloin steak, sliced into thin strips

1 tablespoon olive oil

1 tablespoon butter (use vegan butter or ghee for dairy-free
or paleo options)

1 onion, finely chopped

2 cloves garlic, minced

8 ounces sliced mushrooms

1 cup beef broth (use vegetable broth for vegetarian/vegan
option)

1 tablespoon Dijon mustard

1 tablespoon Worcestershire sauce (use gluten-free
Worcestershire sauce for gluten-free option)

1/2 cup sour cream (use dairy-free sour cream for dairy-free
option)

Salt and pepper, to taste

8 ounces egg noodles or pasta (use gluten-free pasta for
gluten-free option)

Directions:

Heat the olive oil and butter in a large skillet over medium-high heat. Add the sliced beef and cook until browned, about 3-4 minutes per side. Remove the beef from the skillet and set aside.

Add the chopped onion and garlic to the skillet and cook until the onion is translucent, about 2-3 minutes. Add the sliced mushrooms and cook until they are tender, about 5-7 minutes.

Pour the beef broth into the skillet and stir to combine. Add the Dijon mustard and Worcestershire sauce and stir to combine.

Add the cooked beef back into the skillet and let the mixture simmer for 10-15 minutes to allow the flavors to meld together.

While the beef stroganoff is simmering, cook the egg noodles or pasta according to the package directions. Drain and set aside.

Once the beef stroganoff has simmered, remove the skillet from heat and stir in the sour cream until it is fully incorporated. Season with salt and pepper to taste.

Serve the beef stroganoff over the cooked egg noodles or pasta.

Variations:

For a lower-carb option, swap out the egg noodles or pasta for zucchini noodles or spaghetti squash.

For a vegetarian or vegan option, swap out the beef for a plant-based protein such as tofu or tempeh, and use vegetable broth instead of beef broth.

For a dairy-free option, use dairy-free sour cream or coconut cream in place of the regular sour cream.

For a gluten-free option, use gluten-free Worcestershire sauce and gluten-free pasta or zucchini noodles.

Beef Bourguignon

Ingredients:

2 lbs beef chuck roast, cut into 2-inch pieces

2 tablespoons olive oil

Salt and pepper, to taste

4 slices bacon, diced (use turkey bacon for a lower-fat option)

1 onion, finely chopped

2 cloves garlic, minced

2 carrots, peeled and sliced

2 celery stalks, sliced

1 tablespoon tomato paste

2 cups red wine (use beef or vegetable broth for alcohol-free option)

1 1/2 cups beef or vegetable broth

2 bay leaves

1 teaspoon thyme leaves

2 tablespoons cornstarch (use arrowroot powder for paleo option)

1/4 cup cold water

Fresh parsley, chopped (optional)

Directions:

Preheat oven to 350°F.

Heat 2 tablespoons of olive oil in a large dutch oven over medium-high heat.

Season beef chuck roast with salt and pepper, and then brown on all sides in the dutch oven. Remove beef from the dutch oven and set aside.

In the same dutch oven, sauté diced bacon until crispy. Remove bacon from the dutch oven and set aside.

Add onion, garlic, carrots, and celery to the dutch oven, and sauté until onions are translucent.

Add tomato paste to the dutch oven and stir to combine.

Pour in red wine and beef or vegetable broth, stirring to combine. Add in bay leaves and thyme leaves.

Return beef and bacon to the dutch oven, and bring mixture to a simmer.

Cover the dutch oven with a tight-fitting lid and place in the oven. Bake for 2 hours, or until beef is tender.

In a small bowl, whisk together cornstarch and cold water. Remove the dutch oven from the oven and place it on the stove over medium heat.

Pour in the cornstarch mixture, stirring constantly until sauce has thickened.

Remove bay leaves and discard.

Serve Beef Bourguignon hot, garnished with fresh parsley, if desired.

Variations:

For a lower-fat option, use turkey bacon or skip the bacon altogether.

For a vegetarian or vegan option, use mushrooms in place of the beef and vegetable broth instead of beef broth. Add extra vegetables such as pearl onions, turnips, and potatoes to make up for the missing meat.

For a gluten-free option, ensure that your broth and cornstarch or arrowroot powder are gluten-free.

For a paleo option, skip the cornstarch and use arrowroot powder instead. Make sure to use paleo-friendly bacon and broth.

Beef and Mushroom Meatloaf

Ingredients:

1 pound ground beef (use ground turkey or chicken for a lower-fat option)

1 cup finely chopped mushrooms

1/2 cup finely chopped onion

2 cloves garlic, minced

1/2 cup almond flour (use gluten-free breadcrumbs for gluten-free option)

1/4 cup milk (use unsweetened almond milk for dairy-free option)

1 egg

1 tablespoon Worcestershire sauce (use gluten-free Worcestershire sauce for gluten-free option)

1 teaspoon dried thyme

1 teaspoon salt

1/2 teaspoon black pepper

1/4 cup ketchup (use sugar-free ketchup for a low-carb option)

2 tablespoons brown sugar (use coconut sugar for paleo option)

1 tablespoon mustard

Directions:

Preheat oven to 350°F.

In a large mixing bowl, combine ground beef, chopped mushrooms, onion, and garlic.

In a separate bowl, mix together almond flour, milk, egg, Worcestershire sauce, thyme, salt, and black pepper.

Add the almond flour mixture to the beef mixture and mix until well combined.

Transfer the mixture to a 9x5-inch loaf pan and smooth the top.

In a small bowl, whisk together ketchup, brown sugar, and mustard.

Spread the ketchup mixture over the top of the meatloaf.

Bake in preheated oven for 60-70 minutes, or until the internal temperature reaches 160°F.

Let the meatloaf rest for 5-10 minutes before slicing and serving.

Variations:

For a lower-fat option, use ground turkey or chicken in place of the ground beef.

For a gluten-free option, use gluten-free breadcrumbs instead of almond flour.

For a dairy-free option, use unsweetened almond milk in place of regular milk.

For a low-carb option, use sugar-free ketchup.

For a paleo option, use coconut sugar instead of brown sugar and ensure that your Worcestershire sauce and ketchup are paleo-friendly.

Beef Goulash

Ingredients:

2 lbs beef chuck roast, cut into 1-inch cubes

2 tablespoons olive oil

2 onions, chopped

2 cloves garlic, minced

2 tablespoons paprika (use smoked paprika for a smoky flavor)

1 teaspoon caraway seeds

1 teaspoon dried thyme

2 cups beef broth (use vegetable broth for a vegetarian/vegan option)

1 can (14.5 oz) diced tomatoes

2 bell peppers, chopped

1 tablespoon cornstarch (use arrowroot powder for a paleo option)

2 tablespoons cold water

Salt and pepper, to taste

Fresh parsley, chopped (optional)

Directions:

Heat olive oil in a large dutch oven over medium-high heat.

Add beef cubes to the dutch oven and brown on all sides. Remove beef from the dutch oven and set aside.

Add onions and garlic to the dutch oven, and sauté until onions are translucent.

Add paprika, caraway seeds, and thyme to the dutch oven, stirring to combine.

Pour in beef broth and diced tomatoes, stirring to combine.

Return beef to the dutch oven, and bring mixture to a simmer.

Cover the dutch oven with a tight-fitting lid and simmer over low heat for 1 1/2 to 2 hours, or until beef is tender.

Add chopped bell peppers to the dutch oven, and continue to simmer for another 15-20 minutes, or until bell peppers are tender.

In a small bowl, whisk together cornstarch and cold water. Remove the dutch oven from heat and place it on the stove over medium heat.

Pour in the cornstarch mixture, stirring constantly until sauce has thickened.

Season with salt and pepper, to taste.

Serve Beef Goulash hot, garnished with fresh parsley, if desired.

Variations:

For a vegetarian/vegan option, use vegetable broth in place of beef broth and add additional vegetables such as diced potatoes or mushrooms.

For a lower-fat option, use a leaner cut of beef or skip the meat altogether and use only vegetables.

For a gluten-free option, ensure that your broth and cornstarch or arrowroot powder are gluten-free.

For a paleo option, use arrowroot powder instead of cornstarch and make sure your broth is paleo-friendly.

Beef and Potato Casserole

Ingredients:

1 lb ground beef (use ground turkey or chicken for a lower-fat option)

1 onion, chopped

3 cloves garlic, minced

2 cups chopped potatoes

1 cup chopped carrots

1 cup chopped celery

1 cup beef broth (use vegetable broth for a vegetarian/vegan option)

1 can (14.5 oz) diced tomatoes

1 teaspoon dried thyme

1 teaspoon dried rosemary

Salt and pepper, to taste

1/4 cup grated cheddar cheese (use dairy-free cheese for a dairy-free option)

Directions:

Preheat oven to 375°F.

In a large skillet, brown the ground beef over medium-high heat until fully cooked. Drain any excess fat.

Add chopped onion and garlic to the skillet, and sauté until onion is translucent.

Add chopped potatoes, carrots, celery, beef broth, diced tomatoes, thyme, and rosemary to the skillet. Season with salt and pepper, to taste. Stir to combine.

Bring the mixture to a boil, then reduce heat to low and let simmer for 10-15 minutes, or until vegetables are tender.

Transfer the mixture to a 9x13-inch baking dish.

Sprinkle grated cheddar cheese on top of the mixture.

Bake in preheated oven for 15-20 minutes, or until cheese is melted and bubbly.

Let the casserole cool for 5-10 minutes before serving.

Variations:

For a lower-fat option, use ground turkey or chicken in place of the ground beef.

For a vegetarian/vegan option, use vegetable broth in place of beef broth and skip the cheese or use a dairy-free cheese.

For a gluten-free option, ensure that your broth and any other ingredients used are gluten-free.

For a paleo option, skip the cheese and ensure that your broth and all other ingredients used are paleo-friendly.

Spaghetti Bolognese

Ingredients:

1 lb ground beef (use ground turkey or chicken for a lower-fat option)

1 onion, chopped

2 cloves garlic, minced

1 can (14.5 oz) diced tomatoes

1 can (6 oz) tomato paste

1 cup beef broth (use vegetable broth for a vegetarian/vegan option)

1 tablespoon dried oregano

1 tablespoon dried basil

Salt and pepper, to taste

1 lb spaghetti (use gluten-free spaghetti for a gluten-free option)

Fresh parsley, chopped (optional)

Directions:

In a large skillet, brown the ground beef over medium-high heat until fully cooked. Drain any excess fat.

Add chopped onion and garlic to the skillet, and sauté until onion is translucent.

Add diced tomatoes, tomato paste, beef broth, oregano, basil, salt, and pepper to the skillet. Stir to combine.

Bring the mixture to a boil, then reduce heat to low and let simmer for 20-30 minutes, stirring occasionally.

While the sauce is simmering, cook the spaghetti according to package instructions.

Serve the spaghetti topped with the Bolognese sauce. Garnish with fresh parsley, if desired.

Variations:

For a lower-fat option, use ground turkey or chicken in place of the ground beef.

For a vegetarian/vegan option, use vegetable broth in place of beef broth and skip the meat or use a plant-based meat alternative.

For a gluten-free option, ensure that your spaghetti and any other ingredients used are gluten-free.

For a paleo option, skip the spaghetti and ensure that your broth and all other ingredients used are paleo-friendly. Serve the Bolognese sauce over zucchini noodles or spaghetti squash.

Beef Brisket

Ingredients:

1 (5-6 pound) beef brisket, trimmed of excess fat

2 tablespoons kosher salt

1 tablespoon freshly ground black pepper

2 tablespoons smoked paprika

2 tablespoons garlic powder

2 tablespoons onion powder

2 tablespoons dried thyme

2 cups beef broth

1 cup red wine

2 onions, sliced

4 cloves garlic, smashed

4 carrots, peeled and chopped

4 stalks celery, chopped

2 bay leaves

2 tablespoons olive oil

Directions:

Preheat the oven to 350°F.

In a small bowl, mix together the kosher salt, black pepper, smoked paprika, garlic powder, onion powder, and dried thyme to make a dry rub.

Rub the dry rub all over the beef brisket, making sure to coat it well on all sides.

Heat the olive oil in a large Dutch oven or heavy pot over medium-high heat.

Once hot, sear the brisket for 3-4 minutes per side until it develops a nice crust. Remove the brisket and set it aside.

In the same pot, add the onions, garlic, carrots, and celery. Sauté for 5-6 minutes until the vegetables begin to soften.

Pour in the beef broth and red wine, and add the bay leaves. Bring to a boil.

Return the brisket to the pot, and spoon some of the liquid over the top.

Cover the pot with a tight-fitting lid and place it in the preheated oven. Cook for 3-4 hours, or until the brisket is tender and falls apart easily with a fork.

Remove the brisket from the pot and let it rest for 10-15 minutes before slicing against the grain.

Strain the remaining liquid and vegetables to make a sauce to serve with the brisket.

Enjoy your delicious Beef Brisket!

Note: This recipe can be modified to fit various dietary needs. For example, you can use low-sodium beef broth, skip the wine or use a non-alcoholic substitute, and adjust the seasonings to your taste. You can also add more vegetables or use different ones, such as mushrooms or bell peppers, to make the dish more colorful and nutritious.

Philly Cheesesteak

Ingredients:

1 pound thinly sliced beef sirloin or ribeye steak (use portobello mushrooms or seitan for a vegetarian/vegan option)

4 hoagie rolls (use gluten-free rolls for a gluten-free option)

1 onion, sliced

1 green bell pepper, sliced

8 slices provolone cheese (use dairy-free cheese for a dairy-free option)

2 tablespoons olive oil

Salt and pepper, to taste

Directions:

Heat the olive oil in a large skillet over medium-high heat.

Add the sliced onion and green bell pepper to the skillet, and sauté until the vegetables are tender and lightly browned.

Add the thinly sliced beef to the skillet, and season with salt and pepper. Cook for 2-3 minutes until the beef is browned on all sides and cooked through. (If using mushrooms or seitan, sauté them until tender and lightly browned instead.)

Preheat the broiler on high.

Split the hoagie rolls in half and place them on a baking sheet.

Place a slice of provolone cheese on the bottom half of each roll.

Spoon the beef and vegetable mixture over the cheese, dividing it evenly among the rolls.

Top each roll with another slice of provolone cheese.

Broil the sandwiches in the oven for 1-2 minutes, or until the cheese is melted and bubbly.

Serve hot and enjoy your delicious Philly Cheesesteak sandwiches!

Variations:

For a vegetarian/vegan option, use portobello mushrooms or seitan in place of the beef, and use dairy-free cheese.

For a gluten-free option, use gluten-free hoagie rolls or serve the beef and vegetable mixture over a bed of rice or quinoa.

For a low-carb option, skip the hoagie rolls and serve the beef and vegetable mixture over a bed of lettuce or as a bowl with cauliflower rice.

For a spicy option, add some sliced jalapeños or red pepper flakes to the beef and vegetable mixture.

Beef Shawarma

Ingredients:

1 pound beef sirloin, thinly sliced (use tofu or seitan for a vegetarian/vegan option)

1/4 cup olive oil

2 tablespoons lemon juice

2 cloves garlic, minced

1 teaspoon ground cumin

1 teaspoon smoked paprika

1/2 teaspoon ground coriander

Salt and pepper, to taste

Pita bread or lettuce leaves (use gluten-free wraps or lettuce leaves for a gluten-free option)

Sliced tomatoes, cucumbers, and onions, for serving

Tzatziki sauce or hummus, for serving (use dairy-free or vegan alternatives for dietary needs)

Directions:

In a large bowl, whisk together the olive oil, lemon juice, garlic, cumin, smoked paprika, coriander, salt, and pepper.

Add the sliced beef to the bowl and toss to coat evenly in the marinade. Cover and refrigerate for at least 2 hours, or overnight for best results.

Preheat the oven to 400°F (200°C) and line a baking sheet with parchment paper.

Arrange the marinated beef on the prepared baking sheet in a single layer. Bake for 10-15 minutes, or until cooked through and lightly browned.

While the beef is baking, prepare your choice of wrap or lettuce leaves for serving.

Top the wrap or lettuce with sliced tomatoes, cucumbers, and onions.

Once the beef is done, remove it from the oven and let it rest for a few minutes.

Slice the beef thinly and add it to the wrap or lettuce leaves.

Top with a dollop of tzatziki sauce or hummus and serve.

Variations:

For a vegetarian/vegan option, use tofu or seitan instead of beef.

For a gluten-free option, use gluten-free wraps or lettuce leaves instead of pita bread.

For a low-carb option, use lettuce leaves as a wrap and serve with a side of cauliflower rice or roasted vegetables.

For a spicy option, add some chili flakes or hot sauce to the marinade.

Mongolian Beef

Ingredients:

1 pound flank steak, sliced against the grain into thin strips (use tofu or tempeh for a vegetarian/vegan option)

1/4 cup cornstarch (use arrowroot or potato starch for a gluten-free option)

1/4 cup vegetable oil

1/4 cup soy sauce (use tamari or coconut aminos for a gluten-free and/or soy-free option)

1/4 cup brown sugar (use coconut sugar or maple syrup for a lower glycemic index)

1 tablespoon rice vinegar

2 cloves garlic, minced

1 teaspoon ginger, minced

1/4 teaspoon red pepper flakes (optional)

Sliced green onions and sesame seeds, for garnish

Directions:

In a large bowl, toss the sliced beef with the cornstarch until the beef is coated evenly.

Heat the vegetable oil in a large skillet or wok over high heat. Once the oil is hot, add the beef and cook until browned and crispy, about 2-3 minutes per side. Remove the beef from the skillet and set it aside on a plate.

In the same skillet, reduce the heat to medium and add the soy sauce, brown sugar, rice vinegar, garlic, ginger, and red pepper flakes (if using). Cook for 2-3 minutes, stirring constantly, until the sauce thickens.

Add the beef back to the skillet and toss to coat evenly in the sauce. Cook for an additional 1-2 minutes to heat the beef through.

Serve the Mongolian beef hot, garnished with sliced green onions and sesame seeds.

Variations:

For a vegetarian/vegan option, use tofu or tempeh instead of beef.

For a gluten-free option, use arrowroot or potato starch instead of cornstarch, and use tamari or coconut aminos instead of soy sauce.

For a lower glycemic index option, use coconut sugar or maple syrup instead of brown sugar.

For a spicier option, increase the amount of red pepper flakes or add some sliced chili peppers to the dish.

Corned Beef and Cabbage

Ingredients:

4-5 pounds corned beef brisket (use a vegan/vegetarian alternative if desired)

1 onion, quartered

4 cloves garlic, smashed

2 bay leaves

1 teaspoon black peppercorns

1 head of cabbage, cut into wedges

6-8 small red or yellow potatoes, halved (use sweet potatoes for a lower-carb option)

3 large carrots, peeled and cut into chunks

1 cup chicken or vegetable broth (use water or vegetable broth for a vegan option)

1 tablespoon whole grain mustard (use a gluten-free mustard if needed)

Salt and pepper, to taste

Directions:

Preheat the oven to 325°F (160°C).

In a large Dutch oven or pot, place the corned beef brisket, onion, garlic, bay leaves, and peppercorns. Add enough water to cover the brisket by about an inch.

Bring the water to a simmer over medium heat. Once simmering, cover the pot with a lid and transfer it to the oven. Cook for 2-3 hours, or until the beef is fork-tender.

Remove the pot from the oven and transfer the brisket to a cutting board. Let it rest for 10-15 minutes before slicing it against the grain into thin strips.

While the beef is resting, add the cabbage, potatoes, and carrots to the pot with the cooking liquid. If needed, add more water to just cover the vegetables.

Bring the liquid to a simmer over medium heat and cook until the vegetables are tender, about 20-30 minutes.

Remove the vegetables from the pot with a slotted spoon and transfer them to a serving platter. Arrange the sliced beef on top of the vegetables.

In a small bowl, whisk together the broth and mustard. Pour the mixture over the beef and vegetables.

Season with salt and pepper to taste, and serve hot.

Variations:

For a vegetarian/vegan option, use a vegetarian/vegan corned beef alternative and vegetable broth instead of chicken broth.

For a gluten-free option, use a gluten-free mustard.

For a lower-carb option, use sweet potatoes instead of regular potatoes.

For a spicier option, add some sliced jalapenos or red pepper flakes to the cooking liquid.

Beef Wellington:

Ingredients:

1 pound beef tenderloin (use a vegan/vegetarian alternative if desired)

Salt and pepper, to taste

1 tablespoon olive oil

1/2 onion, chopped

2 cloves garlic, minced

8 ounces mushrooms, finely chopped

1/4 cup dry white wine (use vegetable broth or water for a non-alcoholic option)

1/4 cup chopped walnuts (use almond flour or breadcrumbs for a nut-free option)

1/2 teaspoon dried thyme

1 sheet puff pastry (use a gluten-free alternative if needed)

1 egg, beaten (use a vegan egg substitute if desired)

Directions:

Preheat the oven to 425°F (218°C).

Season the beef tenderloin with salt and pepper to taste.

Heat the olive oil in a skillet over medium-high heat. Add the beef and sear on all sides until browned. Remove from the skillet and set aside to cool.

In the same skillet, add the onion, garlic, and mushrooms. Cook until the mushrooms have released their liquid and the mixture is dry.

Add the white wine and cook until the liquid has evaporated. Stir in the walnuts and thyme, and season with salt and pepper to taste.

Roll out the puff pastry on a floured surface. Place the mushroom mixture in the center of the pastry, leaving enough space on the sides to fold over the beef.

Place the beef on top of the mushroom mixture, and fold the pastry over the beef, pressing the edges to seal.

Brush the beaten egg over the top of the pastry to create a golden brown finish.

Place the beef Wellington on a baking sheet and bake in the preheated oven for 35-40 minutes, or until the pastry is golden brown and the beef is cooked to your desired level of doneness.

Remove from the oven and let the beef Wellington rest for 10 minutes before slicing and serving.

Variations:

For a vegetarian/vegan option, use a vegetarian/vegan alternative for the beef tenderloin and omit the foie gras.

For a nut-free option, use almond flour or breadcrumbs instead of walnuts.

For a gluten-free option, use gluten-free puff pastry.

For a non-alcoholic option, use vegetable broth or water instead of white wine.

Steak Diane

Ingredients:

2 (6-ounce) beef tenderloin steaks (use a vegan/vegetarian alternative if desired)

Salt and pepper, to taste

1 tablespoon olive oil

2 tablespoons unsalted butter (use a vegan/vegetarian butter substitute if desired)

1/4 cup chopped shallots

2 cloves garlic, minced

1/4 cup cognac (use vegetable broth or water for a non-alcoholic option)

1/2 cup beef broth (use vegetable broth for a vegetarian/vegan option)

2 tablespoons Dijon mustard (use a gluten-free alternative if needed)

1/4 cup heavy cream (use coconut cream or non-dairy milk for a dairy-free option)

2 tablespoons chopped fresh parsley leaves for garnish

Directions:

Season the beef tenderloin steaks with salt and pepper to taste.

Heat the olive oil in a skillet over medium-high heat. Add the steaks and sear on both sides until browned. Remove from the skillet and set aside.

In the same skillet, add the butter, shallots, and garlic. Cook until the shallots are soft and translucent.

Add the cognac and cook until the liquid has reduced by half.

Add the beef broth and Dijon mustard, and whisk to combine. Cook until the sauce has thickened slightly.

Reduce the heat to low and stir in the heavy cream. Cook until the sauce has thickened and coats the back of a spoon.

Return the steaks to the skillet and cook until the steaks are cooked to your desired level of doneness.

Serve the steaks with the sauce spooned over the top, and garnish with chopped parsley.

Variations:

For a vegetarian/vegan option, use a vegetarian/vegan alternative for the beef tenderloin and omit the cream and butter. Use coconut cream or non-dairy milk instead of heavy cream, and a vegan/vegetarian butter substitute instead of regular butter.

For a gluten-free option, use a gluten-free Dijon mustard.

For a non-alcoholic option, use vegetable broth or water instead of cognac.

Beef Carpaccio

Ingredients:

1 pound beef tenderloin, trimmed of fat

Salt and pepper, to taste

2 tablespoons olive oil

1 tablespoon lemon juice

1 tablespoon capers

Optional garnishes: shaved Parmesan cheese, arugula, sliced cherry tomatoes

For gluten-free: make sure to use gluten-free capers and check the labels of other optional garnishes for gluten-containing ingredients.

For dairy-free: omit the Parmesan cheese or use a dairy-free alternative.

For low-carb: skip the optional garnishes or use low-carb options like sliced avocado or cucumber.

Instructions:

Freeze the beef tenderloin for 30 minutes to make it easier to slice thinly.

Using a sharp knife, slice the beef into very thin slices and arrange them on a platter.

Season the beef slices with salt and pepper to taste.

In a small bowl, whisk together the olive oil, lemon juice, and capers.

Drizzle the dressing over the beef slices and garnish with shaved Parmesan cheese, arugula, and sliced cherry tomatoes, if desired.

Serve immediately.

Braised Short Ribs

Ingredients:

4 lbs beef short ribs

Salt and pepper, to taste

2 tablespoons olive oil

1 onion, chopped

2 carrots, chopped

2 celery stalks, chopped

4 cloves garlic, minced

2 cups beef broth

1 cup red wine

2 tablespoons tomato paste

2 bay leaves

Optional garnishes: chopped fresh parsley, sliced scallions

For gluten-free: make sure to use gluten-free beef broth and check the labels of other ingredients for gluten-containing ingredients.

For low-carb: skip the mashed potatoes and serve with roasted vegetables or cauliflower mash.

For paleo: omit the red wine and replace with additional beef broth or bone broth.

Instructions:

Preheat oven to 325°F.

Season the short ribs with salt and pepper to taste.

In a large Dutch oven, heat the olive oil over medium-high heat.

Sear the short ribs on all sides until browned, about 3-4 minutes per side.

Remove the short ribs from the pot and set aside.

Add the onion, carrots, celery, and garlic to the pot and sauté until softened, about 5 minutes.

Stir in the beef broth, red wine, tomato paste, and bay leaves.

Return the short ribs to the pot and spoon the sauce over them.

Cover the pot with a lid and transfer it to the oven.

Bake for 2.5-3 hours, or until the short ribs are tender and falling off the bone.

Remove the pot from the oven and let it cool for a few minutes.

Discard the bay leaves and skim any fat from the surface of the sauce.

Serve the short ribs with the sauce spooned over them, and garnish with chopped fresh parsley and sliced scallions, if desired.

Prime Rib Roast

Ingredients:

1 (4 to 5 lb.) bone-in prime rib roast

Salt and pepper, to taste

3-4 cloves of garlic, minced

2 tbsp. of fresh herbs (rosemary, thyme, parsley), chopped

2 tbsp. of olive oil

Optional modifications:

For a gluten-free version, use a gluten-free seasoning blend or substitute the herbs with your preferred gluten-free options.

For a dairy-free version, skip the butter or substitute with a non-dairy alternative.

For a lower sodium version, reduce the amount of salt used or use a salt substitute.

Instructions:

Preheat the oven to 450°F (230°C).

Remove the prime rib roast from the fridge and let it sit at room temperature for at least 30 minutes.

In a small bowl, mix together the minced garlic, chopped herbs, and olive oil.

Season the prime rib roast with salt and pepper to taste.

Rub the garlic and herb mixture all over the prime rib roast, making sure to coat it evenly.

Place the prime rib roast in a roasting pan, fat side up.

Roast the prime rib for 15 minutes at 450°F (230°C) to sear the outside.

Reduce the oven temperature to 325°F (160°C) and continue cooking for 15-20 minutes per pound for a medium-rare roast, or until the internal temperature reaches 120-130°F (50-55°C) on a meat thermometer.

Remove the prime rib roast from the oven and let it rest for 10-15 minutes before carving.

Optional modifications:

For a keto version, omit the olive oil and use butter or ghee instead.

For a paleo version, use coconut oil or avocado oil instead of olive oil.

For a whole30 version, use ghee or clarified butter instead of regular butter and make sure the seasoning blend is whole30 compliant.

Serve the prime rib roast with your preferred sides, such as roasted vegetables, mashed potatoes, or a salad. Enjoy!

Dessert

Fruit Salad

Coconut Milk Pudding

Chocolate Avocado Mousse

Chia Seed Pudding

Berry Crisp

Banana Oat Cookies

Baked Apples

Rice Pudding

Sorbet

Pumpkin Pie

Chocolate Chip Cookies

Carrot Cake:

Fudge

Lemon Bars

Ice Cream

Cheesecake

Peanut Butter Cups

Apple Crumble

Tiramisu

Chocolate Truffles

Fruit Sorbet Floats

Chocolate Mousse

Lemon Meringue Pie

Pecan Pie Bars

Cinnamon Sugar Donuts

Fruit Salad

Ingredients:

2 cups of chopped mixed fruit (e.g. apples, strawberries, grapes, pineapple, mango, etc.)

1/4 cup of freshly squeezed orange juice

1 tablespoon of honey or maple syrup (use agave syrup if vegan)

1/4 teaspoon of ground cinnamon (optional)

1/4 cup of chopped nuts (e.g. almonds, pecans, or walnuts; omit if nut-free)

Fresh mint leaves for garnish (optional)

Instructions:

Wash and chop your choice of mixed fruit into bite-sized pieces.

In a small bowl, whisk together the orange juice, honey/maple syrup, and cinnamon (if using).

Pour the orange juice mixture over the chopped fruit and toss to coat evenly.

Sprinkle the chopped nuts over the top of the fruit salad.

Garnish with fresh mint leaves, if desired.

Notes:

To make this fruit salad vegan, use maple syrup or agave syrup instead of honey.

If you have any dietary restrictions or allergies, you can easily customize this recipe by using fruits and nuts that suit your needs.

For a low-sugar version, you can omit the honey/maple syrup altogether and just use the orange juice to sweeten the fruit salad.

You can also add other ingredients such as shredded coconut, chia seeds, or granola for extra texture and flavor.

This fruit salad can be served immediately, or it can be chilled in the refrigerator for a few hours before serving.

Coconut Milk Pudding

Ingredients:

1 can of full-fat coconut milk

2 tablespoons of cornstarch

2 tablespoons of sugar or other sweetener of your choice (e.g. honey, maple syrup, stevia)

1/4 teaspoon of vanilla extract

A pinch of salt

Optional toppings: fresh fruit, nuts, shredded coconut, chocolate chips, etc.

Instructions:

In a small bowl, whisk together the cornstarch, sugar, vanilla extract, and salt.

In a medium-sized saucepan, heat the coconut milk over medium heat until it comes to a simmer.

Add the cornstarch mixture to the saucepan and whisk constantly for 1-2 minutes, or until the mixture thickens and coats the back of a spoon.

Remove the saucepan from heat and pour the mixture into individual serving dishes or a large bowl.

Allow the pudding to cool to room temperature, then refrigerate for at least 2 hours to set.

Top with your choice of toppings before serving.

Notes:

To make this pudding vegan or dairy-free, use a plant-based milk such as almond or soy milk instead of the coconut milk.

For a lower-sugar version, you can reduce the amount of sugar or use a sugar substitute such as stevia or monk fruit sweetener.

This recipe is also gluten-free, but be sure to check the label of your cornstarch to ensure it is gluten-free.

You can experiment with different flavors by adding spices such as cinnamon or cardamom, or by using different extracts such as almond or coconut extract.

This pudding can be stored in the refrigerator for up to 3 days.

Chocolate Avocado Mousse

Ingredients:

2 ripe avocados

1/2 cup of unsweetened cocoa powder

1/2 cup of non-dairy milk (e.g. almond milk, coconut milk, soy milk)

1/4 cup of sweetener of your choice (e.g. maple syrup, honey, agave nectar, stevia)

1 teaspoon of vanilla extract

A pinch of salt

Optional toppings: fresh berries, nuts, shredded coconut, whipped cream, etc.

Instructions:

Cut the avocados in half, remove the pit, and scoop the flesh into a food processor or blender.

Add the cocoa powder, non-dairy milk, sweetener, vanilla extract, and salt to the food processor or blender.

Process or blend the mixture until it is smooth and creamy.

Taste the mixture and adjust the sweetness as needed.

Transfer the mixture to individual serving dishes or a large bowl.

Chill the mousse in the refrigerator for at least 1 hour before serving.

Top with your choice of toppings before serving.

Notes:

To make this mousse vegan or dairy-free, use a non-dairy milk such as almond, coconut, or soy milk.

For a lower-sugar version, you can reduce the amount of sweetener or use a sugar substitute such as stevia or monk fruit sweetener.

You can experiment with different flavors by adding spices such as cinnamon or cayenne pepper, or by using different extracts such as almond or peppermint extract.

This mousse can be stored in the refrigerator for up to 3 days.

If you don't have a food processor or blender, you can mash the avocados by hand and mix the ingredients together with a whisk or fork. The texture won't be as smooth, but it will still taste delicious!

Chia Seed Pudding

Ingredients:

1/2 cup of chia seeds

2 cups of non-dairy milk (e.g. almond milk, coconut milk, soy milk)

1/4 cup of sweetener of your choice (e.g. maple syrup, honey, agave nectar, stevia)

1 teaspoon of vanilla extract

Optional toppings: fresh fruit, nuts, shredded coconut, chocolate chips, etc.

Instructions:

In a mixing bowl, whisk together the chia seeds, non-dairy milk, sweetener, and vanilla extract.

Cover the bowl and refrigerate for at least 2 hours, or overnight, until the mixture thickens and the chia seeds soften.

Whisk the mixture again to ensure the chia seeds are evenly distributed.

Transfer the mixture to individual serving dishes or a large bowl.

Top with your choice of toppings before serving.

Notes:

To make this pudding vegan or dairy-free, use a non-dairy milk such as almond, coconut, or soy milk.

For a lower-sugar version, you can reduce the amount of sweetener or use a sugar substitute such as stevia or monk fruit sweetener.

You can experiment with different flavors by adding spices such as cinnamon or cardamom, or by using different extracts such as almond or coconut extract.

This pudding can be stored in the refrigerator for up to 5 days.

If you prefer a smoother texture, you can blend the mixture in a blender or food processor before refrigerating.

For a thicker pudding, you can use more chia seeds. For a thinner pudding, you can use less chia seeds or more non-dairy milk.

Berry Crisp

Ingredients:

For the filling:

4 cups of mixed berries (such as blueberries, raspberries, blackberries)

2 tablespoons of cornstarch or arrowroot powder

1/4 cup of sweetener of your choice (e.g. maple syrup, honey, agave nectar, stevia)

1 tablespoon of lemon juice

1 teaspoon of vanilla extract

For the topping:

1 cup of rolled oats

1/2 cup of almond flour or other gluten-free flour

1/2 cup of chopped nuts (such as almonds or pecans)

1/4 cup of sweetener of your choice (e.g. maple syrup, honey, agave nectar, stevia)

1/4 cup of coconut oil or other oil of your choice

1 teaspoon of cinnamon

1/4 teaspoon of salt

Instructions:

Preheat the oven to 350°F (180°C).

In a mixing bowl, combine the berries, cornstarch or arrowroot powder, sweetener, lemon juice, and vanilla extract. Mix well and transfer the mixture to a baking dish.

In another mixing bowl, combine the rolled oats, almond flour or other gluten-free flour, chopped nuts, sweetener, coconut oil or other oil of your choice, cinnamon, and salt. Mix well until the mixture is crumbly.

Spread the crumble mixture over the berry mixture in the baking dish.

Bake for 30-40 minutes, until the topping is golden brown and the filling is bubbly.

Remove from the oven and let cool for a few minutes before serving.

Serve warm, topped with your choice of whipped cream, ice cream, or yogurt.

Notes:

To make this Berry Crisp vegan or dairy-free, use coconut oil instead of butter and non-dairy whipped cream, ice cream, or yogurt.

For a lower-sugar version, you can reduce the amount of sweetener or use a sugar substitute such as stevia or monk fruit sweetener.

You can use any combination of berries you like, or substitute with other fruits such as peaches or apples.

For a nut-free version, you can omit the chopped nuts and use more oats or flour.

You can experiment with different spices and extracts to customize the flavor to your liking.

Banana Oat Cookies

Ingredients:

2 ripe bananas, mashed

1 1/2 cups of rolled oats

1/4 cup of nut butter (e.g. almond butter, peanut butter)

1/4 cup of sweetener of your choice (e.g. maple syrup, honey, agave nectar, stevia)

1 teaspoon of vanilla extract

Optional mix-ins: chocolate chips, chopped nuts, dried fruit, etc.

Instructions:

Preheat the oven to 350°F (180°C) and line a baking sheet with parchment paper.

In a mixing bowl, combine the mashed bananas, rolled oats, nut butter, sweetener, and vanilla extract. Mix well until all ingredients are evenly combined.

Fold in any optional mix-ins you choose, such as chocolate chips, chopped nuts, or dried fruit.

Scoop spoonfuls of the mixture onto the prepared baking sheet and flatten them slightly with a fork.

Bake for 15-20 minutes, until the cookies are golden brown and set.

Remove from the oven and let cool on the baking sheet for a few minutes before transferring to a wire rack to cool completely.

Serve and enjoy!

Notes:

To make these cookies vegan or dairy-free, use a non-dairy nut butter such as almond or peanut butter, and use a vegan sweetener such as maple syrup or agave nectar.

For a lower-sugar version, you can reduce the amount of sweetener or use a sugar substitute such as stevia or monk fruit sweetener.

You can use any nut butter you like, or substitute with sunflower seed butter for a nut-free version.

These cookies can be stored in an airtight container for up to 5 days.

You can experiment with different mix-ins and flavorings to customize the cookies to your liking.

For a gluten-free version, make sure to use certified gluten-free rolled oats.

Baked Apples

Ingredients:

4 large apples, cored

1/4 cup of chopped nuts (such as almonds or pecans)

1/4 cup of raisins or dried cranberries

1/4 cup of sweetener of your choice (e.g. maple syrup, honey, agave nectar, stevia)

1 teaspoon of cinnamon

1/4 teaspoon of nutmeg

1/4 cup of water

Optional toppings: whipped cream, yogurt, or ice cream

Instructions:

Preheat the oven to 375°F (190°C).

In a mixing bowl, combine the chopped nuts, raisins or dried cranberries, sweetener, cinnamon, and nutmeg. Mix well.

Stuff each cored apple with the nut mixture, packing it tightly.

Place the stuffed apples in a baking dish and pour water around the apples.

Bake for 30-40 minutes, until the apples are tender and the filling is golden brown.

Remove from the oven and let cool for a few minutes before serving.

Serve warm, topped with your choice of whipped cream, yogurt, or ice cream.

Notes:

To make this recipe vegan or dairy-free, use a non-dairy sweetener such as maple syrup or agave nectar, and use a non-dairy whipped cream or yogurt for the topping.

For a lower-sugar version, you can reduce the amount of sweetener or use a sugar substitute such as stevia or monk fruit sweetener.

You can experiment with different nuts and dried fruit to customize the filling to your liking.

For a nut-free version, you can omit the nuts and use more dried fruit or oats in the filling.

You can also add other spices such as ginger or cloves to the filling for extra flavor.

For a gluten-free version, make sure to use certified gluten-free oats in the filling.

Rice Pudding

Ingredients:

1 cup of white rice, rinsed and drained

2 cups of water

2 cups of milk of your choice (e.g. whole milk, almond milk, coconut milk)

1/4 cup of sweetener of your choice (e.g. sugar, maple syrup, honey, stevia)

1 teaspoon of vanilla extract

Optional mix-ins: raisins, chopped nuts, cinnamon, nutmeg

Instructions:

In a medium saucepan, combine the rice and water. Bring to a boil over medium-high heat, then reduce the heat to low and simmer, covered, for 18-20 minutes, until the water is absorbed and the rice is tender.

Add the milk, sweetener, and vanilla extract to the saucepan with the rice. Stir well to combine.

Cook the rice pudding over medium heat, stirring frequently, for 10-15 minutes, until the mixture thickens and the rice is creamy.

Stir in any optional mix-ins you choose, such as raisins, chopped nuts, cinnamon, or nutmeg.

Remove the rice pudding from the heat and let cool for a few minutes.

Serve warm or chilled, garnished with additional mix-ins if desired.

Notes:

To make this recipe vegan or dairy-free, use a non-dairy milk such as almond milk or coconut milk, and use a vegan sweetener such as maple syrup or agave nectar.

For a lower-sugar version, you can reduce the amount of sweetener or use a sugar substitute such as stevia or monk fruit sweetener.

You can experiment with different spices and mix-ins to customize the rice pudding to your liking.

For a gluten-free version, make sure to use certified gluten-free rice.

Mango Sorbet:

Ingredients:

2 ripe mangoes, peeled and cubed

1/2 cup water

1/2 cup sugar

2 tablespoons lime juice

Instructions:

In a small saucepan, combine the water and sugar. Heat over medium heat, stirring occasionally, until the sugar is completely dissolved.

Place the mango cubes and lime juice in a blender or food processor. Pulse until smooth.

Add the simple syrup (sugar and water mixture) to the blender and blend again until fully incorporated.

Pour the mixture into a shallow dish or ice cream maker and freeze until solid, stirring occasionally.

Serve scoops of the mango sorbet in bowls or cones and enjoy!

Dietary variations:

For a vegan option, replace the sugar with a vegan sweetener such as agave nectar or maple syrup.

For a low-carb option, replace the sugar with a low-carb sweetener such as stevia or erythritol.

For a gluten-free option, make sure to use gluten-free ingredients.

For a dairy-free option, make sure to use water instead of milk or cream.

Pumpkin Pie

Ingredients:

1 1/2 cups pumpkin puree

1/2 cup sugar

1/2 teaspoon salt

1 teaspoon ground cinnamon

1/2 teaspoon ground ginger

1/4 teaspoon ground cloves

2 large eggs

1 can (12 ounces) evaporated milk

1 unbaked 9-inch pie crust

Instructions:

Preheat the oven to 425°F.

In a large mixing bowl, combine the pumpkin puree, sugar, salt, cinnamon, ginger, and cloves. Mix well.

Beat the eggs in a separate bowl and add them to the pumpkin mixture. Stir until fully combined.

Gradually add in the evaporated milk, stirring until the mixture is smooth.

Pour the mixture into the pie crust and smooth the top with a spatula.

Bake for 15 minutes at 425°F, then reduce the oven temperature to 350°F and continue baking for an additional 40-50 minutes, or until a knife inserted in the center comes out clean.

Remove the pie from the oven and let it cool to room temperature before serving.

Dietary variations:

For a vegan option, use a vegan pie crust and replace the eggs and evaporated milk with a vegan egg substitute and a non-dairy milk such as almond milk.

For a low-carb option, replace the sugar with a low-carb sweetener such as stevia or erythritol.

For a gluten-free option, use a gluten-free pie crust and make sure to use gluten-free ingredients.

For a dairy-free option, replace the evaporated milk with a non-dairy milk such as almond milk or coconut milk.

Chocolate Chip Cookies

Ingredients:

1 cup all-purpose flour (or gluten-free flour blend for gluten-free option)

1/2 teaspoon baking soda

1/4 teaspoon salt

1/2 cup unsalted butter, softened (or vegan butter for vegan option)

1/2 cup granulated sugar

1/2 cup brown sugar

1 egg (or flax egg for vegan option)

1 teaspoon vanilla extract

1 cup dairy-free chocolate chips (or regular chocolate chips if dairy is not a concern)

Directions:

Preheat the oven to 350°F (180°C). Line a baking sheet with parchment paper.

In a small bowl, whisk together the flour, baking soda, and salt.

In a large bowl, beat the butter, granulated sugar, and brown sugar together until creamy.

Beat in the egg (or flax egg) and vanilla extract until well combined.

Gradually add the flour mixture to the butter mixture, mixing until just combined.

Fold in the chocolate chips.

Using a cookie scoop or spoon, drop rounded balls of dough onto the prepared baking sheet.

Bake for 10-12 minutes, or until the edges are lightly golden.

Let the cookies cool on the baking sheet for a few minutes, then transfer them to a wire rack to cool completely.

Variations:

For a gluten-free option, use a gluten-free flour blend instead of all-purpose flour.

For a vegan option, use vegan butter and a flax egg instead of regular butter and egg.

For a lower sugar option, use a sugar substitute like stevia or monk fruit sweetener instead of granulated and brown sugar.

For a dairy-free option, use dairy-free chocolate chips instead of regular chocolate chips.

Carrot Cake:

Ingredients:

2 cups all-purpose flour (or gluten-free flour blend)

2 teaspoons baking powder

1 1/2 teaspoons baking soda

1 teaspoon ground cinnamon

1/2 teaspoon ground ginger

1/2 teaspoon ground nutmeg

1/2 teaspoon salt

1 1/2 cups granulated sugar (or coconut sugar)

1 cup vegetable oil (or applesauce for a lower-fat option)

4 large eggs (or flax eggs for a vegan option)

2 teaspoons vanilla extract

3 cups grated carrots

1 cup chopped walnuts (optional)

For the Frosting:

1/2 cup unsalted butter, at room temperature (or vegan butter for a vegan option)

8 ounces cream cheese, at room temperature (or vegan cream cheese for a vegan option)

1 teaspoon vanilla extract

3 cups powdered sugar (or powdered sugar alternative, such as Swerve)

Instructions:

Preheat oven to 350°F. Grease and flour a 9-inch cake pan or line with parchment paper.

In a medium bowl, whisk together the flour, baking powder, baking soda, cinnamon, ginger, nutmeg, and salt until well combined.

In a large bowl, beat together the sugar, oil, eggs, and vanilla extract until well combined.

Add the dry ingredients to the wet ingredients and stir until just combined.

Fold in the grated carrots and chopped walnuts (if using).

Pour the batter into the prepared cake pan and bake for 35-40 minutes or until a toothpick inserted into the center comes out clean.

Allow the cake to cool completely before frosting.

To make the Frosting:

In a large bowl, beat the butter until smooth.

Add the cream cheese and vanilla extract, and beat until well combined.

Gradually add the powdered sugar, beating until the frosting is light and fluffy.

Frost the cooled cake as desired.

Dietary Variations:

Gluten-Free: Use a gluten-free flour blend instead of all-purpose flour.

Vegan: Use flax eggs instead of regular eggs, applesauce instead of oil, and vegan cream cheese and butter for the frosting.

Lower-Fat: Use applesauce instead of oil in the cake batter.

Low-Sugar: Use a sugar alternative such as coconut sugar or Swerve in place of granulated sugar in the cake batter, and use a sugar alternative in the frosting as well.

Fudge

Ingredients:

2 cups granulated sugar

3/4 cup unsweetened cocoa powder

1 cup almond milk (for vegan option) or whole milk (for non-vegan option)

1/4 cup coconut oil (for vegan option) or butter (for non-vegan option)

1 tsp vanilla extract

Pinch of salt

Optional add-ins:

Chopped nuts (pecans, walnuts, almonds)

Dried fruit (cranberries, cherries, raisins)

Mini marshmallows (for a rocky road variation)

Crushed candy canes (for a festive holiday variation)

Directions:

Line an 8x8 inch baking dish with parchment paper.

In a medium saucepan, combine the sugar, cocoa powder, almond milk (or whole milk), and coconut oil (or butter) over medium heat. Stir continuously until the mixture is smooth and well-combined.

Increase the heat to high and bring the mixture to a boil, stirring constantly.

Reduce the heat to medium-low and continue to stir for another 5-7 minutes, until the mixture thickens and becomes glossy.

Remove the pan from the heat and stir in the vanilla extract and salt. If adding any optional mix-ins, stir them in at this point.

Pour the fudge mixture into the prepared baking dish and smooth out the top with a spatula.

Allow the fudge to cool at room temperature for at least 2 hours, or until it has set.

Once the fudge has set, remove it from the baking dish and cut it into small squares.

Dietary variations:

For a vegan option, use almond milk instead of whole milk and coconut oil instead of butter.

For a gluten-free option, make sure all ingredients used are certified gluten-free.

For a dairy-free option, use almond milk and coconut oil instead of whole milk and butter.

For a lower sugar option, reduce the amount of sugar to 1 1/2 cups and add 1/2 cup of unsweetened applesauce to the mixture.

Lemon Bars

Ingredients:

1 cup all-purpose flour (or gluten-free flour)

1/2 cup almond flour

1/2 cup powdered sugar

1/2 cup butter (or dairy-free butter substitute)

2 large eggs

3/4 cup granulated sugar (or alternative sweetener like stevia or erythritol)

1/4 cup fresh lemon juice

1 tablespoon lemon zest (optional)

2 tablespoons cornstarch (or arrowroot powder for a gluten-free option)

1/2 teaspoon baking powder

Pinch of salt

Instructions:

Preheat the oven to 350°F (175°C). Line an 8x8 inch baking dish with parchment paper or grease with cooking spray.

In a mixing bowl, combine the all-purpose flour, almond flour, powdered sugar, and salt. Add in the butter and mix until crumbly.

Press the mixture evenly into the bottom of the prepared baking dish.

Bake for 20-25 minutes or until golden brown. Remove from the oven and let cool slightly.

While the crust is cooling, prepare the lemon filling. In a separate bowl, whisk together the eggs, granulated sugar, lemon juice, lemon zest, cornstarch, baking powder, and salt until well combined.

Pour the filling over the cooled crust.

Bake for an additional 20-25 minutes or until the filling is set and no longer jiggly.

Remove from the oven and let cool completely before slicing into bars.

Optional: Dust with additional powdered sugar or top with whipped cream (or whipped coconut cream for a dairy-free option) before serving.

Ice Cream

Ingredients:

2 cans full-fat coconut milk

1/2 cup granulated sugar (or sweetener of choice)

1/4 cup agave syrup (or maple syrup)

2 tsp vanilla extract

Pinch of salt

For Chocolate ice cream:

1/3 cup cocoa powder

For Strawberry ice cream:

1 cup fresh strawberries, pureed

For Nutella ice cream:

1/2 cup Nutella

For Matcha green tea ice cream:

2 tbsp matcha green tea powder

Instructions:

In a medium-sized saucepan, combine coconut milk, sugar, agave syrup, vanilla extract, and salt. Cook over medium heat, whisking occasionally, until the sugar is dissolved.

For chocolate ice cream: whisk in cocoa powder until fully combined.

For strawberry ice cream: whisk in pureed strawberries until fully combined.

For Nutella ice cream: whisk in Nutella until fully combined.

For Matcha green tea ice cream: whisk in matcha powder until fully combined.

Transfer the mixture to a blender and blend until smooth.

Chill the mixture in the refrigerator for at least 4 hours, or overnight.

Pour the mixture into an ice cream maker and churn according to manufacturer's instructions, usually around 25-30 minutes.

Transfer the ice cream to a container and freeze for a few hours to firm up.

Enjoy your homemade, delicious, and dietary-friendly ice cream!

Cheesecake

Ingredients:

1 1/2 cups graham cracker crumbs (or gluten-free cookie crumbs for a gluten-free version)

1/4 cup unsalted butter, melted (or coconut oil for a dairy-free version)

4 (8-ounce) packages cream cheese, at room temperature (or vegan cream cheese for a vegan version)

1 cup granulated sugar (or coconut sugar for a refined sugar-free version)

4 large eggs, at room temperature (or flax eggs for a vegan version)

1 teaspoon vanilla extract

1/2 cup sour cream (or dairy-free sour cream for a dairy-free version)

Toppings of your choice, such as fruit or chocolate chips (choose according to your dietary needs)

Instructions:

Preheat the oven to 325°F (160°C).

In a medium bowl, mix together the graham cracker crumbs and melted butter until the mixture is moistened.

Press the mixture into the bottom of a 9-inch springform pan, using the bottom of a glass to help flatten it.

In a large bowl, beat the cream cheese and sugar with an electric mixer until creamy and smooth.

Add the eggs, one at a time, beating well after each addition.

Stir in the vanilla extract and sour cream until well combined.

Pour the cheesecake mixture into the prepared crust.

Bake for 50-60 minutes or until the center of the cheesecake is almost set.

Turn off the oven and leave the cheesecake in the oven with the door slightly open for 30 minutes.

Remove the cheesecake from the oven and let it cool completely at room temperature.

Once cooled, refrigerate the cheesecake for at least 4 hours or overnight before serving.

Top with your desired toppings before serving.

Peanut Butter Cups

Ingredients:

1 cup creamy peanut butter (or almond butter for a lower carb option)

1/4 cup honey (or sugar-free sweetener for a keto option)

1/2 cup coconut flour (or almond flour for a gluten-free option)

1/4 tsp salt

1/2 cup sugar-free chocolate chips (or dark chocolate chips for a vegan option)

Instructions:

In a mixing bowl, combine the peanut butter, honey (or sweetener), coconut flour (or almond flour), and salt. Mix well until a dough-like consistency is formed.

Line a mini muffin tin with paper liners. Take small pieces of the dough and press them into the bottom and sides of the paper liners to form a cup.

Melt the chocolate chips in the microwave or on a double boiler. Spoon a small amount of melted chocolate into each cup, making sure to cover the bottom and sides of the cup.

Place the muffin tin in the freezer for 10-15 minutes to allow the chocolate to harden.

Spoon a small amount of peanut butter mixture into each cup, leaving a little room at the top.

Pour the remaining melted chocolate over the peanut butter, making sure to cover the top and seal the cup.

Place the muffin tin in the freezer for an additional 10-15 minutes to allow the chocolate to harden.

Once the peanut butter cups are completely frozen, remove them from the muffin tin and store in an airtight container in the freezer.

Note: This recipe can be modified to fit various dietary needs. You can use almond butter instead of peanut butter for a lower carb option, or use sugar-free sweetener instead of honey for a keto option. You can also use almond flour instead of coconut flour for a gluten-free option, and dark chocolate chips instead of sugar-free chocolate chips for a vegan option.

Apple Crumble

Ingredients:

6 medium apples, peeled and sliced

1/4 cup granulated sugar

1/4 cup brown sugar

1 tsp cinnamon

1/2 tsp nutmeg

1/2 cup all-purpose flour (use gluten-free flour for a gluten-free option)

1/2 cup old-fashioned oats

1/2 cup almond flour (use coconut flour for a nut-free option)

1/2 cup melted butter (use vegan butter for a vegan option)

1/4 cup chopped nuts (optional)

Directions:

Preheat the oven to 375°F (190°C) and grease an 8x8 inch baking dish.

In a large bowl, mix together the sliced apples, granulated sugar, brown sugar, cinnamon, and nutmeg. Transfer the mixture to the prepared baking dish.

In a separate bowl, mix together the flour, oats, almond flour, and melted butter until well combined. Stir in the chopped nuts, if using.

Spread the crumble mixture evenly over the apples.

Bake for 40-45 minutes or until the top is golden brown and the apples are tender.

Serve warm with vanilla ice cream or whipped cream, if desired.

Note: To make this recipe lower in sugar, you can reduce the amount of sugar or use a sugar substitute such as stevia or erythritol. To make it dairy-free, use a dairy-free butter alternative.

Tiramisu

Ingredients:

6 egg yolks

3/4 cup granulated sugar

2/3 cup milk

1 1/4 cups heavy cream

1/2 cup mascarpone cheese (cream cheese)

1/4 cup brandy

1/4 cup coffee liqueur (such as Kahlua)

2 cups strong brewed coffee, cooled to room temperature

1 package ladyfingers (about 24-28 cookies)

Cocoa powder for dusting

Instructions:

In a large mixing bowl, beat the egg yolks and sugar together until light and fluffy.

In a saucepan, heat the milk over medium heat until it begins to simmer. Gradually whisk the hot milk into the egg yolk mixture.

Return the mixture to the saucepan and cook over medium heat, stirring constantly, until it thickens and coats the back of a spoon. Remove from heat and let cool to room temperature.

In a separate bowl, whip the heavy cream until stiff peaks form. In another bowl, beat the mascarpone cheese until smooth. Fold the whipped cream into the mascarpone cheese.

Gently fold the cooled egg mixture into the whipped cream and mascarpone cheese mixture.

In a shallow dish, mix together the brandy, coffee liqueur, and brewed coffee. Dip each ladyfinger into the coffee mixture, making sure to coat both sides. Place the soaked ladyfingers in a single layer in the bottom of an 8x8 inch baking dish.

Spread half of the cream mixture over the ladyfingers. Dip the remaining ladyfingers into the coffee mixture and layer them on top of the cream mixture. Spread the remaining cream mixture over the ladyfingers.

Cover the dish with plastic wrap and refrigerate for at least 4 hours, or overnight.

When ready to serve, dust the top of the Tiramisu with cocoa powder.

Varation:

Ingredients:

6 egg yolks

3/4 cup granulated sugar

2/3 cup milk

1 1/4 cups heavy cream

1/2 cup mascarpone cheese (cream cheese)

1/4 cup amaretto liqueur

2 cups strong brewed coffee, cooled to room temperature

1 package ladyfingers (about 24-28 cookies)

Cocoa powder for dusting

Instructions:

In a large mixing bowl, beat the egg yolks and sugar together until light and fluffy.

In a saucepan, heat the milk over medium heat until it begins to simmer. Gradually whisk the hot milk into the egg yolk mixture.

Return the mixture to the saucepan and cook over medium heat, stirring constantly, until it thickens and coats the back of a spoon. Remove from heat and let cool to room temperature.

In a separate bowl, whip the heavy cream until stiff peaks form. In another bowl, beat the mascarpone cheese until smooth. Fold the whipped cream into the mascarpone cheese.

Gently fold the cooled egg mixture into the whipped cream and mascarpone cheese mixture.

In a shallow dish, mix together the amaretto liqueur and brewed coffee. Dip each ladyfinger into the coffee mixture, making sure to coat both sides. Place the soaked ladyfingers in a single layer in the bottom of an 8x8 inch baking dish.

Spread half of the cream mixture over the ladyfingers. Dip the remaining ladyfingers into the coffee mixture and layer them on top of the cream mixture. Spread the remaining cream mixture over the ladyfingers.

Cover the dish with plastic wrap and refrigerate for at least 4 hours, or overnight.

When ready to serve, dust the top of the Tiramisu with cocoa powder.

*** personally I will use combine both the amaretto and the coffee liquor .

Varation

Ingredients:

2 cups strong brewed coffee, cooled to room temperature

2 packages of gluten-free ladyfingers (about 24-28 cookies)

1 cup raw cashews, soaked in water overnight

1/2 cup full-fat coconut cream

1/4 cup coconut oil, melted

1/4 cup maple syrup

2 teaspoons vanilla extract

Pinch of salt

1-2 tablespoons cocoa powder for dusting

Instructions:

Start by making the dairy-free filling. Drain the soaked cashews and rinse them well. Place them in a high-speed blender along with the coconut cream, melted coconut oil, maple syrup, vanilla extract, and salt. Blend until smooth and creamy, scraping down the sides as needed. Set aside.

Pour the cooled coffee into a shallow dish. Dip the gluten-free ladyfingers into the coffee, one at a time, and arrange them in a single layer in the bottom of an 8x8 inch baking dish. You may need to break some of the ladyfingers in half to fit them in the dish.

Spoon half of the dairy-free filling on top of the ladyfingers and spread it into an even layer. Repeat with another layer of coffee-dipped ladyfingers, followed by the remaining filling.

Cover the dish with plastic wrap and chill in the refrigerator for at least 4 hours or overnight.

When ready to serve, dust the top of the Tiramisu with cocoa powder. Cut into squares and serve chilled.

Chocolate Truffles:

Ingredients:

1/2 cup coconut oil, melted

1/2 cup cocoa powder

1/4 cup maple syrup or agave nectar

1/2 tsp vanilla extract

Pinch of sea salt

Optional toppings: shredded coconut, chopped nuts, cocoa powder

Directions:

In a mixing bowl, whisk together the melted coconut oil, cocoa powder, maple syrup or agave nectar, vanilla extract, and sea salt until smooth and well combined.

Cover the bowl and place it in the fridge for about 30 minutes, or until the mixture has hardened slightly and is easier to handle.

Use a small cookie scoop or spoon to scoop out about 1 tablespoon of the mixture and roll it into a ball.

Roll the ball in your desired toppings, if using, and place it on a parchment-lined baking sheet.

Repeat with the remaining mixture until you have formed all of the truffles.

Place the baking sheet in the fridge and chill the truffles for at least 30 minutes, or until they are firm.

Store the truffles in an airtight container in the fridge for up to a week.

Variations:

For a nut-free version, omit any nut-based toppings and use shredded coconut or cocoa powder instead.

For a lower sugar version, reduce the amount of maple syrup or agave nectar and use a natural sweetener like stevia or monk fruit sweetener instead.

For a different flavor profile, add in a teaspoon of cinnamon or cardamom to the mixture before rolling into balls.

Fruit Sorbet Floats

Ingredients:

2 cups fruit sorbet (flavor of your choice)

2 cups sparkling water or soda (flavor of your choice)

Fresh fruit for garnish (optional)

Instructions:

Scoop the sorbet into a tall glass.

Slowly pour the sparkling water or soda over the sorbet, making sure not to overflow the glass.

Gently stir the sorbet and sparkling water/soda together with a spoon.

Add fresh fruit on top for garnish, if desired.

Serve immediately and enjoy!

Variations:

For a dairy-free option, use a dairy-free sorbet such as coconut sorbet or soy-based sorbet.

For a sugar-free option, use a sugar-free sorbet or substitute the soda with a sugar-free flavored sparkling water.

For a low-carb option, use a low-carb sorbet or substitute the soda with a sugar-free flavored sparkling water.

For a boozy option, add a splash of your favorite spirit such as vodka or rum to the sorbet before pouring the sparkling water/soda on top.

Chocolate Mousse:

Ingredients:

1 can of full-fat coconut milk, chilled overnight

1/2 cup of dairy-free chocolate chips

2 tbsp of maple syrup

1 tsp of vanilla extract

Pinch of sea salt

Instructions:

Remove the can of coconut milk from the fridge and flip it upside down. Open the can and pour out the liquid, leaving only the solidified coconut cream at the bottom of the can.

In a small saucepan, melt the chocolate chips over low heat, stirring frequently.

In a mixing bowl, whisk the coconut cream until it becomes smooth and fluffy.

Add the melted chocolate, maple syrup, vanilla extract, and sea salt to the mixing bowl. Mix everything together until it's well combined and the mixture is creamy and smooth.

Pour the mixture into small serving bowls or ramekins and refrigerate for at least 2 hours or until set.

Serve chilled, garnished with fresh berries or coconut whipped cream if desired.

Optional variations:

To make it nut-free, you can use dairy-free chocolate chips that are made without nuts or substitute the chocolate with carob chips.

To make it sugar-free, you can use sugar-free chocolate chips and replace the maple syrup with a natural sugar substitute like stevia or erythritol.

To make it paleo-friendly, use paleo-friendly chocolate chips and replace the maple syrup with honey.

Lemon Meringue Pie

Ingredients:

For the crust:

1 1/4 cups gluten-free flour blend

1/4 teaspoon salt

1/2 cup dairy-free butter, chilled and cubed

2-3 tablespoons ice water

For the filling:

1 cup fresh lemon juice

1 tablespoon lemon zest

1/2 cup maple syrup

1/2 cup cornstarch

1/4 teaspoon salt

1 1/2 cups water

4 egg yolks

1/4 cup dairy-free butter

For the meringue:

4 egg whites

1/2 cup sugar

1/2 teaspoon cream of tartar

Directions:

Preheat oven to 350°F (175°C).

In a large bowl, whisk together the gluten-free flour blend and salt. Add the chilled, cubed dairy-free butter and use a pastry cutter or your fingers to work the butter into the flour until the mixture is crumbly.

Gradually add ice water, 1 tablespoon at a time, and stir until the dough comes together into a ball.

Roll the dough out into a 12-inch circle on a floured surface. Carefully transfer the dough to a 9-inch pie dish and trim the edges as needed. Prick the bottom of the crust with a fork and bake for 10-12 minutes, until lightly golden.

In a medium saucepan, whisk together the lemon juice, lemon zest, maple syrup, cornstarch, salt, and water until smooth. Cook over medium heat, stirring constantly, until the mixture thickens and comes to a boil.

In a separate bowl, beat the egg yolks. Gradually add a spoonful of the hot lemon mixture to the eggs, whisking constantly, to temper them. Then pour the egg mixture back into the saucepan and whisk until well combined.

Add the dairy-free butter to the lemon mixture and stir until melted and well combined. Pour the lemon filling into the prepared pie crust.

In a large bowl, beat the egg whites and cream of tartar until soft peaks form. Gradually add the sugar, a spoonful at a time, and continue to beat until stiff peaks form.

Spoon the meringue over the lemon filling, spreading it to the edges of the crust and creating peaks with a spoon or spatula.

Bake the pie for 10-12 minutes, until the meringue is lightly golden. Let cool before serving.

Optional: you can also use a handheld torch to lightly toast the meringue for a classic look and flavor.

Pecan Pie Bars

Ingredients:

2 cups gluten-free flour blend

1/2 cup coconut oil, softened

1/4 cup maple syrup

1/4 teaspoon salt

3 cups pecans, roughly chopped

1/2 cup coconut sugar

1/2 cup maple syrup

1/2 cup coconut cream

2 tablespoons coconut oil

1/2 teaspoon vanilla extract

Pinch of salt

Directions:

Preheat the oven to 350°F (175°C) and line a 9x13 inch baking pan with parchment paper.

In a mixing bowl, combine the gluten-free flour blend, coconut oil, maple syrup, and salt until a crumbly dough forms.

Press the dough into the prepared baking pan and bake for 15-20 minutes, until golden brown.

In a separate mixing bowl, whisk together the coconut sugar, maple syrup, coconut cream, coconut oil, vanilla extract, and salt.

Fold in the chopped pecans and pour the mixture over the baked crust.

Bake for an additional 25-30 minutes, until the filling is set and the edges are golden brown.

Let cool completely before slicing and serving.

This recipe can be modified to fit various dietary needs by substituting the gluten-free flour blend with a different type of flour or flour substitute, and adjusting the sweetener and fat sources to fit your dietary preferences.

Cinnamon Sugar Donuts

Ingredients:

2 cups almond flour

1/4 cup tapioca flour

1/4 cup coconut sugar

1 tsp baking powder

1/2 tsp baking soda

1/2 tsp cinnamon

1/4 tsp salt

1/2 cup almond milk

1/4 cup applesauce

1/4 cup melted coconut oil

1 tsp vanilla extract

1/4 cup granulated sugar

1 tsp cinnamon

Instructions:

Preheat the oven to 350°F (175°C). Lightly grease a donut pan with non-stick cooking spray.

In a large mixing bowl, whisk together the almond flour, tapioca flour, coconut sugar, baking powder, baking soda, cinnamon, and salt.

In a separate bowl, whisk together the almond milk, applesauce, melted coconut oil, and vanilla extract.

Add the wet ingredients to the dry ingredients and stir until well combined.

Spoon the batter into the prepared donut pan, filling each mold about 2/3 full.

Bake for 15-18 minutes, or until a toothpick inserted into the center of a donut comes out clean.

Allow the donuts to cool for a few minutes before removing them from the pan and transferring them to a wire rack.

In a small bowl, mix together the granulated sugar and cinnamon.

Dip each donut into the cinnamon sugar mixture until coated on all sides.

Serve warm and enjoy!

Note: To make these donuts nut-free, you can substitute almond flour with oat flour or another gluten-free flour substitute of your choice.r.

Potatoes

Sauces